Dark Valleys

Dark Valleys

Foul Deeds Among the South Wales Valleys 1845–2016

Gary Dobbs

PEN & SWORD
TRUE CRIME

First published in Great Britain in 2016 by
Pen & Sword True Crime
an imprint of
Pen & Sword Books Ltd
47 Church Street
Barnsley
South Yorkshire
S70 2AS

ISBN 978 1 47386 178 7

Typeset in Ehrhardt by
Mac Style Ltd, Bridlington, East Yorkshire
Printed and bound in the UK by CPI Group (UK) Ltd,
Croydon, CRO 4YY

Pen & Sword Books Ltd incorporates the imprints of Pen & Sword
Archaeology, Atlas, Aviation, Battleground, Discovery, Family
History, History, Maritime, Military, Naval, Politics, Railways,
Select, Transport, True Crime, and Fiction, Frontline Books, Leo
Cooper, Praetorian Press, Seaforth Publishing and Wharncliffe.

For a complete list of Pen & Sword titles please contact
PEN & SWORD BOOKS LIMITED
47 Church Street, Barnsley, South Yorkshire, S70 2AS, England
E-mail: enquiries@pen-and-sword.co.uk
Website: www.pen-and-sword.co.uk

Contents

Acknowledgments

I am deeply in debt to Roni Wilkinson for commissioning this work in the first place, and I also owe thanks to South Wales Police who have patiently answered many questions during the production of this book. Neil Milkins, author of *Every Mother's Nightmare*, was especially helpful regarding the Harold Jones murders, of which he knows more than most. I also owe much to Mr Milkins for his permission to use several of the photographs from his book.

I would also like to mention the team at Cardiff Library for their help in locating information and tracking down obscure documents. The vast archives of the *South Wales Echo*, *Western Mail* and *Cardiff Times* have also proved invaluable in the research needed for a book such as this.

And finally thanks to the proofing, editing and design teams at Pen and Sword Books who transformed my scribbles into the book you now hold.

Gary Dobbs, 2016

Introduction

The South Wales Valleys, *Cymoedd De Cymru*, are in a constant state of flux. These restless hills stretch from eastern Camarthenshire in the west to western Monmouthshire in the east, and from the Heads of the Valleys in the north to the Vale of Glamorgan and the coastal areas around Swansea and Bridgend. Until industrialisation in the mid-nineteenth century the Valleys were only sparsely inhabited, with secluded farmhouses, hamlets and small villages dotted here and there on a map that largely showed a rugged, mountainous landscape.

With industrialisation came great growth. For instance, in the Rhondda Valley, the most famed of the coal-mining areas, there were fewer than 1,000 souls in 1851, but by 1870 this had increased to 17,000 and by 1911 there were 153,000 people living there. At this time Merthyr Tydfil, situated at the extreme north of the Taff Valley, was the biggest town thanks to its growing iron works. The iron and steel works consumed an incredible amount of coal, and with the increased importance of coal many immigrants came into the valleys to live and work. This resulted in rows upon rows of terraced houses springing up on the mountainsides, seemingly grafted into the valley walls, and soon Cardiff, Swansea and Newport were ranked among the most important coal ports in the world.

The coal industry had been artificially buoyed during the two world wars when demand for good-quality coal grew year on year. However, following the Second World War the decline in coal-mining was a country-wide issue but the South Wales Valleys, the Rhondda in particular, were hit especially hard. The 1947 nationalisation of the coal fields were seen as a way to save the industry but each coming decade saw a continued reduction in output from the Welsh mines. By the mid-twentieth-century, oil had replaced coal as the fuel of choice in many industries, thanks largely to political pressure designed to lessen the country's reliance on coal. There were, however, other factors contributing to the decline of Welsh coal-mining, one of these being under-investment in the industry. Many of the Welsh mines had been sunk during the mid- to late 1800s, which meant that they were far smaller than most modern mines and the method of extracting coal was becoming antiquated. In 1947 there were 15,000 miners employed in the Rhondda alone but by 1984 the valleys had just one single pit still operating and this was in Meardy situated at the head of the Rhondda Fach Valley.

In 1979 when Margaret Thatcher became Prime Minister her free market policies soon clashed with the loss-making, government-owned National Coal Board, and in 1984 the government announced that they were to close many of the coal-mines. This led to a bitter strike which ultimately proved unsuccessful with the result being the virtual destruction of the coal industry. The South Wales Valleys paid a heavy price and since the mid-1980s they have seen some of the highest unemployment rates in the United Kingdom, and this tragic trend continues to the present day.

Today the valleys are once more green as signs of the once-incredible levels of industrialisation vanish beneath the reclaiming hand of nature. But the people of the South Wales Valleys are fiercely proud of the history that has gone before them, keenly aware of the hardships endured by those who have lived and died in years long gone. Today these people continue to face economic hardships but they are aware of the fact that the South Wales Valleys have taken on an iconic status. For many people around the world, the Valleys are the abiding image of Wales itself.

Like anywhere else the history of the South Wales Valleys is coloured in many shades, but it is the darker side of history with which this work is concerned. For this book offers a glimpse into their criminal history.

Murder is the most terrible crime of them all. It is the unlawful killing with malice aforethought of another person. In law it is defined as the premeditated state of mind which distinguishes the crime from other unlawful killings such as manslaughter. However, many of the murders detailed within this book were not in fact premeditated.

Often the killer would find himself or herself driven by an uncontrollable series of events, leading to a tragic and deadly conclusion. Outside influences can and often do result in murder, alcohol and drugs can play a part, as can extreme poverty and that old chestnut, greed. But no matter what the reasons it is a fact that we are all ultimately responsible for our own actions and we must bear the cost when these actions are unlawful.

The cases contained within this book have reasons as varied as the methods of killing – jealousy, greed and revenge are among the motives. Victims are decapitated, strangled, shot, and even drowned. The heartache of a spurned lover can turn to brutal violence, greed can have terrible and unforeseen consequences and in one case the desperation of a thirteen-year-old girl suddenly finding herself a mother leads to the murder of her new-born baby.

So join me in this journey through these dark valleys as we uncover these insalubrious slices of history, all the while aware that these are true cases, involving real people. There is no attempt to sensationalise, to dwell on the lurid details, but rather a respectful telling of the way it was.

Chapter 1

Tommy Twice's Date with the Hangman

Thomas Thomas, known as Tommy Twice, faced retribution when on the tenth day of April 1845 he was publicly hanged at Brecon, then a small agricultural town just north of the Brecon Beacons mountain range. He had been found guilty of the murder and robbery of David Lewis, a butter merchant from Lampeter, who had been travelling with his twelve-year-old son, also named David Lewis. As Thomas climbed the steps to the scaffold, he ignored the crowd, more than 20,000 strong, who had gathered besides the river that ran behind Brecon County Gaol, and kept his head bowed. He was sobbing and just before the white hood was placed over his head he grasped the hands of the prison Chaplin, who stood beside him, and said, 'God bless you for all your kindness'.

At precisely ten o'clock the drop was pulled and a sigh came from the crowd as Thomas Thomas danced on the end of the rope, his legs kicking out violently at thin air, before the executioner, William Calcraft ran beneath the scaffold and swung on the prisoner's legs in order to hasten death. Calcraft was a controversial figure and it was claimed that he employed the short drop method of hanging, the drop being barely three feet and insufficient to break a prisoner's neck, in order to entertain the crowds for the several minutes it would take the prisoner to strangle to death. Many of Calcraft's executions were not documented, but it is believed that he was responsible for 450 hangings during his 45-year career. So well known did he become that grim songs were sung about him, but it is fact that Calcraft had the longest career as a hangman in British history and also used the shortest rope. He had the reputation of being a showman with his executions providing a grim spectacle for the always sizeable crowds that gathered: there are reports of him jumping onto a condemned man's back and riding him as the poor soul's neck finally broke. No less a personage than Thomas Hardy even wrote about one of Calcraft's executions; that of Martha Brown which occurred in 1856. 'I remember what a fine figures she showed against the sky as she hung in the misty rain and how the tight black gown set off her shape as she wheeled half round and back.' So taken with the story of poor Martha Brown was he that Hardy would use her as an inspiration for his novel *Tess of the D'Ubervilles*. And it was largely because of Calcraft's theatrics that public executions would be abolished in 1868, but Calcraft would continue with his trade, carrying out his executions within the privacy of drab prison walls, until his forced retirement in 1874.

Eventually Thomas Thomas was perfectly still, save for the gentle swaying of his body in the wind and someone in the crowd shouted out, 'Three cheers for the hangman.' Then William Calcraft bowed as if he were an actor on a stage before moving off into the gaol to collect his fee.

The event that had brought Thomas Thomas to the sadistic hangman occurred in December of the previous year. Brecon's population was growing with the rapid industrialisation of the surrounding areas, which meant that the traders who travelled to the towns to the villages and valleys made a handsome profit. One such trader

William Calcraft, known as the showman hangman. (*Author's collection*)

was David Lewis, a butter merchant, who, travelling with his son, also David Lewis, had sold many firkins of butter and cheese to the people of the district. He was travelling back to his home in Lampeter with a hefty purse, but he would never see his home again.

In the early hours of a cold December morning, John Lennis, the keeper of the Trecastle Inn, was woken by the sound of a boy crying at the toll gate outside. Lennis dressed and went outside and found that the boy didn't have any money to pay the toll. The boy told Lennis that he had fallen asleep on the cart and when he had awoken his father was missing. The boy was twelve years old and John Lennis took pity on him and told him to come into the house out of the cold. While the boy warmed himself by the fire Lennis made ready his own wagon and told the boy they would set out in the direction he had come from to discover what had happened to his father. They had not travelled far when another wagon approached and the driver told them that a man had been found shot dead on the side of the road. The distraught boy would later identify the body as being that of his father.

The story the boy would later tell the police was that he and his father had been travelling with two carts laden with butter and some cheese to sell to the people in the locality, collecting a tidy sum of money as they went. They had called into the Brecon Barracks and there they had been approached by a man who would be identified as Thomas Thomas. After chatting for some time Mr Lewis and Thomas went into the Bridgend Inn, leaving the boy outside to watch the now-empty carts.

When the men emerged from the inn, David Lewis told his son that the man named Thomas Thomas would be travelling with them, and after lighting lanterns they set out. They had gone a few miles when the boy grew tired and he climbed into the front cart, and was soon asleep while his father and Thomas walked besides the carts.

The next thing the boy knew was that he awoke at the Trecastle East gate only to find that his father and the second cart were missing. With the description and the name of the man Thomas Thomas given to the police, the boy was escorted back to his home in Lampeter by two policemen. They assured the boy that Thomas Thomas was well known in the area and would pay dearly for the murder. The knowledge that the man would face justice for the killing was intended to make the devastated boy feel better, but he remained understandably quiet for the remainder of the journey back to Lampeter.

Thomas was arrested on 8 December 1844 by Superintendent Enoch Gwynne of the Camarthenshire Constabulary who had been drafted into the area to aid in the pursuit of the man. Once Thomas was arrested the investigation would discover that he had purchased two pistols a month previously, and when his home was searched they found the weapons, together with several percussion caps. A purse was also discovered that contained a £5 note and a cheque for the same amount. The cheque was identified as one given to Davis Lewis for some of his butter.

Despite all the evidence, Thomas protested his innocence but he was found guilty by a jury, and the judge donned his black cap as he pronounced sentence. Thomas Thomas would be hanged by the neck until he was dead.

Chapter 2

Jane Lewis and the Tyntyla Farm Mystery

It started with a murder at a remote Welsh farm and ended with a mystery far away in Australia. The brutal killing of 22-year-old Jane Lewis on 2 November 1862 in the Rhondda Valley may be long forgotten, consigned to the grim pages of Welsh criminal history but for months following the murder the eyes of the world were firmly focused on the Welsh mining valley

Jane Lewis, was brutally murdered on a lonely hillside deep in the Rhondda. Her throat had been slashed with such ferocity that the head was almost severed from the body. 'I found a razor with blood on it,' PC Richard Wise would later tell the inquest. 'And a brooch which was untouched by blood. There was also a bonnet, ribbon and collar and all were quite saturated with blood. The collar had been cut in two and the string of the bonnet was also cut through.'

It was a bitterly cold Sunday evening in November 1862 when Jane met her demise. That winter had been particularly bad, even by Welsh valley standards where the winter months often bring snow, with temperatures dropping below zero by late October and refusing to rise above it until well into the following spring. However, by

Murder stone commemorating the killing of Jane Lewis. (*Author's collection*)

the time more clement weather arrived Jane would be dead and buried and the mystery surrounding her quite terrible death persists to the present day. For months afterwards the tragedy focused the attention of the world on the small mining village of Gellidawel and even today, more than a hundred years later, it is still referred to as the Tyntyla Farm Mystery.

Tyntyla Farm sat on the steep slope of Penrhys mountain, overlooking the Rhondda Fawr river and the village of Gellidawel. The valleys below the farm were once heavily wooded from the banks of the river to the towering mountains above, but by 1862 the industrialisation of the Rhondda had deposited houses where trees had once been and the rolling green hills were rapidly turning black from the coal-mining.

Tyntyla Farm, though, was still screened from the growing village of Gellidawel by thick woods. There were two tracks from the farm to the village. The direct route went straight down the mountainside,

Tyntyla Farm during the 1860s. (*Author's collection*)

through the woods, to the village – a distance of 656 yards. The other track, more than twice as long, was used by wagons and followed a much gentler slope along the mountainside. Both tracks emerged onto the valley road next to the Star Inn, which today has been turned into a convenience store.

At the time in question there were a total of eleven people living at Tyntyla Farm. These were the farm's tenant, Thomas Williams, his wife Maria, their six children and three servants, 26-year-old Thomas Edmunds, 15-year-old David Morgan and 22-year-old Jane Lewis. Of the three servants, only Jane, the daughter of Issac and Selina Lewis of Tyncoed, was a blood relative of the Williams family, being Maria's niece.

On the evening of Sunday, 2 November 1862, Jane Lewis left Tyntyla Farm sometime between 5.30 and 5.45 in the evening with the intention of attending the evening service at the Nebo Welsh Baptist Chapel in nearby Ystrad. She would not attend the service and other than her killer, her aunt and the children were the last people to see her alive.

Thomas Williams, Jane's uncle, had left the farmhouse earlier that afternoon to visit a nearby farm from where he too would attend the chapel service before returning to Tyntyla later that evening. Thomas Edmunds would also attend the chapel service and it was stated to police that he had left for the service at least half an hour earlier than Jane. The third servant, David Morgan, was considered too young to attend the chapel service and had spent that afternoon amusing himself in the woods around Tyntyla.

Before leaving for the chapel service Jane had informed her aunt that she planned on meeting her sweetheart, a local man also named Thomas Williams but known as Tom Screens, at the service and that afterwards they would most likely attend a tea party that was being held in the village.

At around 8.30 that night, Thomas Williams of Tyntyla returned home and told his wife that Jane had not attended the chapel service, but neither of them were worried since they assumed that she had gone to the tea party she had spoken of. It was thirty minutes later that Tom Screens turned up looking for Jane, saying he was worried that she had taken off with another man. He gave no reason for his suspicions other than the fact that Jane had not met him as promised at the chapel but he was certainly agitated and appeared frantic to find his sweetheart. Shortly afterwards he left the house in search of Jane and the Williams family retired to bed. This information comes from the police reports and strangely there is no mention of when Thomas Edmunds, who had attended the chapel service, returned to the house.

What is known for certain is that Edmunds was in bed at 11 pm when Maria woke to find that Jane had still not returned. Now the woman started to fear for the safety of her niece and she quickly woke her husband and he, together with Edmunds, took a lantern and went out into the darkness to search for the errant girl.

The two men told police that they first searched the outer farm buildings and then took the direct route down to the village below. They didn't get far, just 180 yards down the mountainside heading towards the Gellidawel, when they found Jane's body. Overcome with shock they both ran down to the village to raise the alarm and when they returned they were accompanied by Henry Norton Davies, a surgeon from the nearby village of Cymmer.

'I saw the body of a female at Tyntyla farm, in the parish of Ystrad. The body was cold and stiff,' Davies would tell the inquest. 'Her throat was cut and her clothes were saturated with blood. On looking at the throat it appeared to be cut from side to side. The whole of the soft parts being cut down to the backbone. The deepest part of the cut was behind and below the right ear. After drawing the skin as close to possible to its natural position and replacing its edges, there appeared three horizontal cuts from left to right The principal, and fatal cut, had completely severed the wind pipe cutting through its second cartilage, the gullet and all of the great vessels and nerves in the front of the neck.'

The police were immediately called for and the scene was attended by PC Richard Wise who later reported that he examined the vicinity of the body and could find no signs of a struggle. A blood-soaked razor was found some two feet from the body and a further five feet away he discovered an open razor case without a drop of blood upon it. It seemed on the surface to be an obvious case of murder, but incredibly the jury at the inquest held a month later would return a verdict of suicide while suffering from temporary insanity, a verdict that caused understandable controversy particularly as a medical report stated that the deceased's fingers on both hands had suffered cuts, the middle finger of the right hand having been cut down to the bone as if the victim had tried to fend off an attacker. The post-mortem had also revealed that Jane Lewis, an unmarried woman, had been ten weeks pregnant. In all three surgeons examined the body – the aforementioned Henry Norton Davies, a Dr Edwards from Cardiff and London pathologist Dr Taylor – and all three men concluded that given the nature of the wounds it was impossible that they were self-inflicted. Still twelve of the fourteen persons on the coroner's jury, presumably suffering from mental illness themselves, would declare to an astounded courtroom that in their considered opinion Jane Lewis had killed herself while suffering temporary insanity. 'We have often thought but never with more reason to believe than now, that Welsh juries must be constituted differently than in other parts of the British Empire. We now have this senseless and unjustifiable findings of the twelve jurymen in the Rhondda Valley murder case,' read an editorial in the *Gwent Star* following the inquest.

The coroner seemed to agree with the newspaper and after taking the advice of the judge in the case, he ignored the opinion of the jury and overturned their decision, instead returning an open verdict. It fell short of stating that Jane Lewis had been unlawfully killed, as was obviously the case, but it did at least question the fact that she had committed suicide which was then seen as a mortal sin.

Initially suspicion fell on Tom Screens, who was known to be romantically involved with Jane and had expressed concerns to her aunt and uncle that she had run off with another man. The razor used in the killing was identified as belonging to Thomas Edmunds and he swore it had been at the farmhouse on the Sunday morning prior to Jane's death, this being verified by both Thomas and Maria Williams. It was thought that Screens had stolen the razor when he had visited the farm in search of Jane but before arresting Screens, PC Wise had examined all of Thomas Edmunds' clothing and found not a single drop of blood. Edmunds could also prove that he had been at the chapel service, and before that he had been in the Star Inn. Given that there were witnesses to place Edmunds at both locations, he had a cast-iron alibi.

The Star Inn today is a busy convenience store. The original building was incorporated into a much bigger one in 1912. (*Author's collection*)

Tom Screens was arrested on suspicion of murder early on the morning following the discovery of Jane's body. When questioned, Screens stated that the last time he had seen Jane had been on the previous Wednesday when she had made arrangements to meet him at the chapel service. When asked about his movements on the fateful evening he told police he had been with friends in the village before going onto the chapel service. Many witnesses backed this up and statements confirmed that Screens had not left the village of Gellidawel until the end of the service. He too had an unshakable alibi.

There was one odd point concerning Screens and that was that when he had visited Tyntyla in search of Jane he had taken the longer route to the farmhouse, and took the same route when he left. This seemed odd, considering that Screens had claimed to be frantic to find Jane, particularly after leaving the farmhouse. Why then had he not taken the shorter of the two routes? This, he claimed, was because of the weather: it had been raining and the steep mountain path would be treacherous. He did not think Jane would have gone that way, though police felt that a man concerned for Jane's safety would have searched both routes. However, the post-mortem, performed by Henry Norton Davies, placed the time of death at between 5.30 and 6 pm, shortly after Jane had left the farm, which meant that Screens was in the clear and he was later released without charge.

Next the police would arrest Thomas Edmunds: indeed he was still in custody when the inquest took place but the case against Edmunds was incredibly weak and hinged solely on the fact that the razor used had belonged to him. Edmunds did admit that several weeks before Jane's death he and she had become lovers, which added validity to Screen's fears that she was involved with another man, but following the inquest Edmunds was also released without charge. Shortly afterwards he left Tyntyla and nothing is known of his life afterwards.

Poor Jane Lewis went to her grave with a question-mark hanging over the cause of her death, but even then further indignities were laid upon the poor girl. Jane was buried several miles away at Ainon Baptist Chapel in Tonyrefail. At the time the chapel was newly built and Jane became the first person to be buried there. Several months later a stone, a murder stone, was placed over the grave. It is not known who commissioned the stone, though there is a glaring mistake on the inscription. The stone claims that Jane had died on 2 December 1862, actually the date of the inquest, when in truth she had been killed a full month earlier in November of that year.

The stone reads:

> In memory of Jane, daughter of Issac and Selina Lewis late of Tyn Coed in the parish of Llanillid who, on the Lord's Day December 2nd 1862 probably fell by cruel hand on Ty'n Tyle farm in the parish of Ystradfodwg, aged 23 years and although her blood is hither-to unavenged attention is directed to the day when light will shon on the mysterious occurrence and guilt will be accorded its just reward.

Note the wording, 'probably fell by cruel hand'. Even in eternity Jane's demise is still raising questions.

The police, though, were convinced the girl had indeed been murdered, despite the open verdict and a month after Jane's death they arrested David Thomas, a man who at times had worked as a labourer at Tyntyla Farm and had been spurned by Jane when he had made romantic moves towards her. The arrest split the small community, with many people subscribing to the suicide theory but others in favour of murder. Nevertheless, David Thomas was brought before the magistrates but the hearing, held at the New Inn in Pontypridd, which lasted for several days and was presided by a Mr Perkins, found that he had no case to answer. The police, however, were not done with the case and they next arrested Thomas Edmunds, the young servant from Tyntyla Farm, but he too was later released due to lack of evidence after an understandable public outcry. The police had no-one else to arrest, and eventually they would cast the case aside in favour of more pressing matters.

And so it remains to this day that the mystery surrounding the death of Jane Lewis has never been satisfactorily explained, but there is still more to this sad story. Several months after the tragic events Tom Screens took up lodgings in Tonyrefail, opposite the chapel where Jane was buried. He reportedly spent long hours at the graveside, simply sitting on the ground and mumbling to his departed sweetheart.

Owen Morgan, a valley journalist who would achieve much fame during his career, wrote, using his bardic name Morien, of meeting Tom Screens in Tonyrefail and described him as 'one half broken man'. When asked by the journalist about the night of Jane's death and specifically why he had taken the longer of the two routes to and from Tyntyla Farm, Screens was reported to have said, 'I can't explain that. But I am glad I did not take the shorter route, had I found Jane I would have likely picked her up and gotten blood on my clothing. They would have surely blamed me then.'

Shortly after meeting with the journalist Screens decided to quit Wales and he emigrated to Australia. A move which prompted yet another postscript to the sad case of Jane Lewis. The South Wales police hold a statement, dated 1902, in their archives from a Mr Richard Packer of Treforest. 'A year or two after the Tyntyla murder, my father and I were residing at a place 20 miles from Ballarat, Australia. One Sunday afternoon, we were both out in our shirt sleeves,' read the statement. 'We observed coming along the road, a man behaving strangely. He was picking up stones, and then throwing them at the doors of houses as he went past. He stopped opposite us and said, "You are Welshmen." I replied, "Yes we are. How come you think so?" He answered, "I guessed it by the flannel of your shirts." Then he asked, "From where in Wales?" I replied, "From Llantrisant, Glamorgan." He then said, "I come from the Rhondda Valley. Did you hear of the murder of Jane Lewis of Tyntyla?" I replied in the affirmative. He then said, "It was I that killed her." We never saw him after nor before, and I have no idea who he was.'

The natural assumption is that this destitute-looking man was in fact Tom Screens but as Mr Packer had no idea of the man's name it could quite as easily have been Thomas Edmunds or even some other man whose name didn't even come into the frame at the time of the murder. And if the man had been Screens did his admission amount to the guilt that he could have prevented the murder, or did he mean that he himself had killed Jane Lewis? So many questions that it seems will never be answered, the Tyntyla mystery is destined to remain forever just that; a mystery.

Chapter 3

The Green-Eyed Monster

'O, beware my lord, of Jealousy. It is the green-eyed monster that doth mock the meat it feeds on', wrote Shakespeare in *Othello*.

Jealousy can indeed be a destructive emotion. A person can, when in the grip of such passion, transform from a caring, hard-working spouse into a homicidal maniac. The burst of madness though is often short-lived but leaves behind long-lasting pain. The cases in this chapter attest to this.

Friday, 21 July 1883 saw a brutal crime occur in the bustling coal-mining community of Cymmer, Porth. A trio of cottages known as Rickard's Row, now long demolished to make way for modern flats, stood alongside the Rickard's Arms public house and it was in the middle of these three cottages that the Davies family resided. The head of the household was Edward Davies, a man described as a quiet, hard-working collier. He was the father of ten children and was twice married. His first marriage left him a widower, his second would leave him a killer.

Although Edward Davies had been described favourably by many who knew him, doubts had been cast over the character of his wife. It was reported that she was devoted to the Salvation Army and spent

Edward Davies as represented in a sketch from *The Western Mail*. (*The Western Mail*)

much of her time at meetings, thus neglecting her domestic duties. For weeks before the tragic event that would result in Edward Davies standing trial for murder, he had been subjected to rumours concerning his wife and Captain Bartley of the Porth branch of the Salvation Army. That he had come to believe his wife was pregnant by the man would prove to be the last straw for Edward Davies.

The afternoon before the murder Mrs Davies was visited at her home by a dressmaker, Miss Sarah Evans, with a view to taking measurements for a dress, something for Sunday best, that Mrs Davies had ordered be made for her. Miss Evans would later tell the court that while she was at the Davies' house, Mr Davies came in, accompanied by one of his sons, and announced that he would not be going to work anymore. A short discussion followed after which Mr Davies sat by the fire, smoking his pipe. He seemed, Miss Evans would tell Morien, the pen name of Owen Morgan, a journalist working for the *Western Mail*, like a man with a troubled mind. It would later emerge that Mr Davies had walked out of his work at the Glyn Colliery earlier that day and when asked by a fellow collier, a Mr Josiah Howells, what was wrong, Mr Davies relied, 'You shall hear another time.' The journalist suggested that Mr Davies had taken, 'a lot of chaffing from fellow workers' over rumours that Mrs Davies was romantically involved with the captain of the Porth branch of the Salvation Army. This was confirmed when Edward Emlyn Davies, eldest son of Edward Davies, told the court that people in the street would call, 'Salvation Army' after his father and that friends in the local public house would tease his father about the same thing.

What happened then is that at around 6.15 on the morning of Friday, 21 July 1893, Mr Davies was sat at the table while his fifteen-year-old daughter, Elizabeth Jane Davies, made breakfast. The young girl had just called her mother from bed when her father went and removed something from the kitchen cupboard and then went upstairs. Only minutes later Elizabeth Jane Davies heard frantic screaming and when she ran to the foot of the stairs she saw her father holding her mother by the head and drawing something across her throat.

'My mother was bleeding from the neck,' the girl would later tell the inquest. 'I went to her and took her by the hand. I pulled her away from my father and we ran from the house. My father followed us to our neighbour, Mrs Flowers's house. My father burst in and chased my mother around the table before catching her and once again drawing his razor across her neck. He had killed her.'

Owen 'Morien' Morgan. (*Welsh Archives*)

After that Davies calmly left the house and went back home where he put on his hat and coat and then went straight to Porth police station to confess to his crime. 'I have cut her throat with a razor,' he told a stunned PC Richard Walters. 'I had thought about doing it before. She is bad with Captain Bartley.'

Davies then handed the policeman the sum of £2 in gold and 9d in silver and asked if the money could be shared out between his children. The policeman told the court that Mr Davies was heavily bloodstained, his waistcoat being quite sodden. The policeman stated that he (Mr Davies) seemed outwardly calm but his eyes held a manic appearance.

The ensuing court case was short. There was no question of guilt but merely motive and it was suggested that Mr Davies was insane at the time of the killing. It was known that he had a silver plate in his head, the result of a mining accident several years previously, and that he had been subjected to merciless teasing about his wife's alleged affair with Captain Bartley. He had even believed that his wife was pregnant by the man, though a post-mortem would reveal that Mrs Davies had not been with child.

Edward Davies would be found guilty of wilful murder, though given his mental state at the time of the killing, he escaped a death sentence and instead spent the rest of his life in a mental institution. Jealousy had indeed destroyed the man's mind, no doubt the many weeks of ribbing he had received from workmates over his wife's alleged infidelity with Captain Bartley had gone some way to contributing to his madness.

An Obsessive Husband

Time after time, throughout the history of criminal justice, jealousy has driven men to commit acts of barbaric cruelty. Such was the case of William Augustus Lacey, a Jamaican-born man living in Pontypridd, who in 1900 killed his wife, also by slitting her throat, though unlike Edward Davies, Lacey swung for his crime and was executed by James and William Billington at Cardiff Gaol.

Lacey had the dubious honour of being the subject of the first Welsh execution of the twentieth century.

William Lacey was a native of Kingston, Jamaica. A well-travelled man, he had spent time in America before settling in Liverpool. He was, however, restless, and a few years later he moved to Merthyr where he took up work in a local colliery and became good friends with a Welshman named Augustus O'Connor. The two men became inseparable and when Lacey, finding coal-mining to an

William Lacey as represented in a sketch for the *Cardiff Times*. (*Cardiff Times*)

arduous, low-paid profession, decided to go to America, O'Connor, although a married man, decided to go with him. O'Connor told his wife he would seek better opportunities for them in America and send for her when he had done so.

Shortly before Christmas 1899 though, Lacey and O'Connor returned to Wales and made for Swansea where O'Connor's wife was staying with her parents at 38 Hoo Street, Port Tennant. Lacey accompanied his friend and it was there that he first met nineteen-year-old Pauline Joseph, the younger sister of O'Connor's wife.

Although the girl was ten years younger than he was, Lacey felt an instant attraction towards this pretty young girl. This was mutual and they soon became close and then intimate. The girl's parents strongly objected, no doubt, given the attitudes of the times, the fact that Lacey was a black man would have been a factor in their refusal to accept the relationship. Mixed marriages were at this time virtually unheard-of and the relationship became the source of much disapproving gossip. However, Pauline was a strong-willed woman and she ignored both her parents, and the loose tongues around the town, and on Easter Tuesday, 1900, she and Lacey were married at Swansea Registry Office. The only people, with the obvious exception of the registrar, present for the ceremony were Augustus and Mary O'Connor.

The couple then moved to Pontypridd where Augustus and Mary O'Connor had now settled at 16 Maritime Terrace and the Laceys lived there until June of that year when they took rooms, one up and one down, at 21 Barry Terrace also in Pontypridd. Lacey soon found work as a labourer at the nearby Tymawr Colliery and the newlyweds settled down for what should have been a long life together.

The relationship, however, was tumultuous and the couple were often heard arguing, largely because Mrs Lacey was by all accounts a very beautiful woman and Lacey was insanely jealous and would go into rages whenever another man so much as glanced her way. He had once told Mary O'Connor, during the aftermath of a particularly fierce argument, that if he couldn't have Pauline then he'd swing for her. The words would turn out to be prophetic.

The Laceys' landlady was Catherine Vaughan, and she would witness many of the arguments between the couple. She would later tell police that these rows, often violent, reached a dreadful conclusion after Mrs Lacey received a letter from her estranged parents, which stated that there would always be a room for her at home. The letter had been delivered late in the afternoon of 4 July 1900 and all that evening the Laceys argued. At around 11 pm that night Catherine Vaughan had to knock the wall that separated her room from the young couple and for the rest of the night they were quiet.

The following morning the argument started up again after Lacey refused to go to work. Mrs Lacey called him bone idle and he said he was remaining at home to keep an eye on her. Once again the Laceys' landlady was witness to this and growing tired of the constant bickering, she left the house to seek peace and quiet at a neighbour's home. It was around 11 am when her next-door neighbour, a Mrs Mary Clee, came and told Catherine that something terrible had happened at her home. She quickly returned to the house, expecting to walk in on yet another argument but the sight that greeted her was much worse. Pauline Lacey lay on her back in a pool of blood, her clothing open at the breast but there was no sign of her husband. Lacy, still holding the bloodstained razor, had walked across the town and presented himself at the police station, where he spoke to PC David Evans.

'I have come to give myself up for killing my wife,' Lacy told the startled policeman and handed over the murder weapon. Lacey was cautioned and then led to a cell while the policeman went to Barry Road to check on the story. Having seen the body, the policeman returned to the station and charged Lacey with murder. The policeman recorded Lacey as saying, 'Pauline had said she would be happier with another man. I loves [sic] my wife. Before any man would have the benefit of

The scene of the crime, 21 Barry Road, as it is today. (*Author's collection*)

her I would rather see her laying in the ground. I did it like a man and give myself up.'

On 7 July the inquest opened and the first witness was the landlady, Catherine Vaughan, who told the courts of the constant arguments between the couple. She said that Lacey had struck his wife more than once and that he suspected she had been unfaithful with her brother-in-law, Augustus O'Connor. She had been present once when the two men had argued over this and Lacey had pulled out his razor. The same razor he had used to later kill his wife.

A statement Lacey had made to the police was then presented to the court. He had changed his story somewhat from what he had originally told PC Evans. In this new version of events Lacey claimed that it was his wife who had grabbed the razor and slit her own throat. She didn't go deep enough though and Lacey claimed she had lain on the floor, begging him to finish her off. He claimed that he had taken the razor from his wife and did she asked, finished her off. Afterwards he had walked to the police station and given himself up, with his confession that he had killed his wife.

Medical evidence was then presented and this was followed by the testimony of Mary Clee, the Laceys' next-door neighbour, who said she had heard shouting coming from the Lacey's on the morning that Pauline Lacey had been killed. She said that she had seen Lacey leaving the house and heading towards the town centre. She had looked through the window of Number 21 at that point and saw Mrs Lacey lying in a pool of blood. It was then that she had gone to get Mrs Vaughan who was at a neighbour's house. Lacey then took to the witness box but he was too distraught to give any evidence in his defence and at one point he clenched his hands together, gazed upwards and yelled, 'Come back to me, Pauline.'

The jury returned a verdict of wilful murder and later that day, Lacey appeared before the judge and the proceedings were adjourned until 11 July, coincidentally the same day that Pauline Lacey was laid to rest in her native Swansea

Lacey was sentenced to death: the fact that he had changed his story must have weighed heavily on the judge's ruling. And despite much public sympathy and calls for clemency the sentence was carried out. On Thursday, 23 August 1900, Lacey was hanged at Cardiff Gaol by James and William Billington.

On the eve of the execution, the famed Welsh journalist Owen 'Morien' Morgan wrote an impassioned plea for Royal clemency, arguing that, 'Lacey worshipped his wife.'

So fond was he of her that this bordered on idolatry. In all countries of Europe degrees of guilt, except in Britain, are taken into account in dealing with a case of murder. Now, are there extenuating circumstances in the history of the crime for which Lacey stands justly condemned? Immediately after the murder, I made on the spot, careful inquiry into all the circumstances preceding the perpetration of the crime, and I shall divest myself of a sense of responsibility by making public what I gleaned. Lacey neglected his work to be with his wife. This infatuation became known to his fellow work-

Lacey meets his Doom.

Execution, the current penalty for murder, was the sad lot of Lacey, the coloured man, of Pontypridd, who, in a fit of passion murdered his wife, a white woman, recently. Petitions for his reprieve had been many, public sympathy with him had been great, and wherever the question of the fitness of the punishment to the crime was raised it was never stated with conscientiousness that the greatest penalty of the law was just retribution in Lacey's case. The press were admitted to the execution, which was a ceremony, naturally, of a most touching nature. Lacey maintained his reason to the last, and was able to walk boldly to the scaffold—that terrible spot which spanned the gulf between two great worlds

Cutting from the *Cardiff Times*.
(*Cardiff Times*)

men who gave him much chaffing, and even made up lies that they themselves had known the woman in an improper way. The simple African [*sic*] was thus driven into a constant state of doubt and suspicion. Pauline could not appreciate the man's intense devotion to herself and there is conclusive evidence that she exercised to the utmost the power she held over her lover to tease him and amuse herself with his paroxysms of jealousy. She, like many women before her, little dreamed of the madness she was causing and the danger to herself and him by her reprehensible conduct. Further, Pauline was tired of Lacey. She had married him after a very short acquaintance, and she was living in isolation and as a semi-prisoner due to her husband's jealousy.

The Spurned Lover

In 1902 jealousy would also motivate Phillip Evans, a one-time Pontypridd policeman, to turn his gun on himself, but not before he had killed his estranged lover, Jane Ann Sadler.

Phillip Evans had left Glamorgan years previously after being thrown out of the police force for unsuitable conduct, and had spent some time living in Ireland before returning to Wales where he struck up a relationship with thirty-year-old Jane Ann Sadler, who had recently separated from her husband. By all accounts they were very fond of each other, but their relationship was doomed when Jane decided that she needed to go back to her husband who remained in the marital home in nearby Porth, and give it another try.

Phillip Evans was distraught and he begged Jane to stay with him, but it was futile; she had made up her mind. On the afternoon of Thursday, 27 March 1902, while her husband was at work, Jane agreed to meet Phillip for one last time. The idea was that they would talk things through and then both of them would move on with their respective lives. For the meeting they chose the Hollybush Inn, which was situated in Hopkinstown, half-way between Porth and Pontypridd. Neither of them were known at the pub and as they wanted their meeting to remain a secret, it seemed the perfect venue.

The Hollybush Inn pictured in 2013, shortly before it was demolished. (*Author's collection*)

At this time in the afternoon the Inn was quiet, with only a few customers enjoying a drink in the bar. The landlord Horatio Rowlands noticed the man and woman come in and watched as they went through to the tap room, where they would be alone. Around five minutes elapsed before the landlord heard two hots come from the room and he ran in to find the woman, Jane Ann Sadler, slumped dead on the settee. Phillip Evans was sat next to her: he was semi-conscious and a revolver lay on the floor at his feet. The landlord quickly locked and bolted the door. He then went to alert both the doctor and the police but before he left the inn another shot rang out. The Hollybush Inn had been the venue for the fatal outcome of a *ménage-à-trois*.

When the authorities arrived, Phillip Evans was still alive, though in a bad condition and after being examined by a doctor, who discovered he had shot himself in the head, he was transported to Porth cottage hospital where he would give a statement to PC Bodger stating that he had killed Jane Ann Sadler with a single shot to the head. The bullet had entered her brain and she would have been killed instantaneously. Evans also stated that he wished to die himself.

The police investigation uncovered the details that led to the tragic event. It turned out that Jane Ann Sadler had been married for sixteen years, but had left her husband several months back and started a relationship with Evans. However, shortly before the shooting, Jane had broken off her relationship with Evans, stating that she would go back to her husband and try and fix the marriage. Evans was said to be both devastated and humiliated and he wouldn't accept that his relationship with the woman was over. He had several times sent flowers to her marital home at Church Street, Porth, and also turned up there whilst drunk, demanding to speak to Jane. It was because of this that Jane had agreed to meet him on the fateful night that he killed her. Phillip Evans, seething from the rejection by his lover, had decided that if he couldn't have her then no-one else would. He had premeditated the murder of Jane as well as his own intended suicide.

An inquest was held at Porth Court and came to the conclusion that Evans had wilfully murdered Mrs Sadler. Upon his recovery, the court decided, he would be charged with wilful murder but Evans would not recover, and almost immediately following the inquest he succumbed to his own self-inflicted injuries at Porth Cottage Hospital. The cause of death was pressure on the brain due to the bullet which was still lodged in his head.

A full inquest followed in which several witnesses were called, including Frank Evans, brother of the deceased man. Frank told the coroner's jury that his brother had some very peculiar traits to his personality, and that he had been deeply in love with the woman he had killed. The jury returned a verdict that Phillip Evans had committed both murder and suicide while insane.

Evans would be buried in secret with a simple prayer as a substitute for the usual Church of England service. Eight policeman, former colleagues of the dead man, acted as pallbearers.

Chapter 4

The Bridgend Hotel Killing

The intent had been robbery, but the end result was murder. The guilty man, Eric Lang, real name Eugene Lorenz, would pay the ultimate price for his crimes when, on 21 December 1904, he was hanged by William Billington and John Ellis at Cardiff Gaol. Such was the interest in the case that when the execution was carried out that there was a crowd, estimated at more than 600 strong, waiting outside the prison walls for the raising of the black flag that signified the deed had been done; that justice had been served.

The scene of the crime was the Bridgend Hotel in Ton Pentre, a small but thriving Rhondda coal-mining community. And it was here that around 11.45 pm on Saturday, 10 September 1904, Mary Jones, commonly called Mini, retired to bed after a busy night at the hotel. Mary was the wife of John Emlyn Jones, the landlord of the hotel and as she climbed into bed beside their baby son, her husband remained downstairs to finish up some business and tidy up the bar. Earlier there had been a good crowd in the bar, which was usual for a Saturday night, and it was gone two in the morning before a weary Mr Jones climbed into bed beside his wife and baby. Their bedroom was at the rear of the hotel, overlooking the yard, and the gaslight outside the window gave the bedroom some illumination. There was also a small night-light on the dressing table so that Mrs Jones would be able to see when she awoke to feed the baby.

The Jones family had until three weeks previously run the Royal Oak Inn, at Pontypridd, but had taken over the Bridgend Hotel after the death of the previous licensee, a Mr F.C. Gould. Mr Jones was a native of Bonvilston near Barry while his wife hailed from the Pontypridd area. The couple had settled well into the Rhondda town of Ton Pentre and were very popular with their customers, most said they were a respectable and well liked couple. Indeed, such was the character of the couple that upon leaving the Royal Oak Hotel they had been presented with an illuminated address by Councillor T. Taylor and several other dignitaries.

The address read:

Presented to Mr and Mrs John Emlyn Jones on the occasion of them leaving the Royal Oak Hotel, Pontypridd. On behalf of a large and influential body of your fellow townsmen and well wishers, in which must be included the members of the United Order of Odd-Fellows (Cilfynydd branch), Cilfynydd Homing Society, Norton Bridge Debating Society, and numerous other friends and admirers, the meeting being ably presided over by Councillor T. Taylor, Councillor W.H. Gronow, Councillor T.B. Evans.

Together with numerous friends and admirers, we, the undersigned, beg your acceptance of this address as a token of the respect and esteem with which you were held while in our district. During the time you have lived among us your geniality and cordial good fellowship have gained you the united respect and good feelings of all of whom you have been connected, and we beg to convey our sincere regret at losing so capable and hospitable a host and hostess. We trust that the future for you may be even more successful than the past. And in conclusion we wish you every blessing that health and prosperity can bring.

At around 3 am Mary woke. At first she though it was Clifford, her baby son who had awoken her but the infant was fast asleep between her and her husband. It was then that the woman noticed the face of a man peering at her from between the bars of the brass frame at the

The scene of the crime. The Bridgend Hotel in 1904. (*Author's collection*)

foot of the bed. Mary screamed but the intruder moved fast and hit her violently across the head with an iron bar that was wrapped up in brown paper. Mary was dazed but she moved and a second blow from the iron bar, no doubt also intended for her head, struck her on the left forearm. By now John had woken, as had the baby who was screaming at the top of his lungs, and he lunged at the man who had invaded their home and struck his wife.

The two men grappled in the bedroom and at one point the intruder threw John Jones against the far wall with such force that the plaster cracked. He then got the man around the throat and tried to throttle him but Mary Jones jumped on his back. The intruder, still holding John Jones, shook Mary off but he lost his balance and both men crashed through the open bedroom doorway to continue their struggle on the landing.

There were other members of staff living in the hotel and Mary called for cellarman John Henry Carpenter who slept in the loft bedroom and he responded by shouting back that he was on his way. But before the young man could even pull his trousers on, the struggle was over and John Jones lay dying in his wife's arms. They were now joined by Katie Richards, niece of Mary Jones, who slept in a room at the front of the hotel and had also been awoken by the noise. Katie and John ran to fetch the local doctor, leaving Mary with her unconscious husband still held in her arms. All the while the baby, unharmed but terrified, screamed uncontrollably.

Dr William Evans Thomas, arrived at the Bridgend Hotel at 3.45 am and immediately pronounced John Jones dead. Shortly afterwards Inspector John Williams of Ton Pentre police station, arrived with several constables, and after speaking with the doctor he made a search of the premises. It was discovered that the intruder had got into the building via a ladder placed at the back of the hotel, which reached to an open window of a lavatory. The window was 13ft from the ground and had a faulty catch so the intruder had been able to remove one of the frames thus making the opening big enough for a man to climb through. Downstairs the cash register had been left open and Mary Jones told the police that no cash would have been left in the till overnight. No doubt the intruder had discovered this and then made his way upstairs. A pair of boots were found at the foot of the stairs and once it was confirmed that these neither belonged to John Jones or John Carpenter, it was reasonable to deduce that they had belonged to the intruder and that he had fled without them.

Back in the bedroom the inspector discovered an iron bar wrapped in brown paper which was smeared with blood. This was the weapon used to first cosh Mr Jones and then used on her husband. Upon examining the dead man, the inspector noted that there were eight cuts on his left hand and a wound on his forearm, just over an inch long. These, of course, were defence wounds and told the inspector of the brutal struggle that had occurred between the two men. The fatal wound, a stab in the left-hand side of Mr Jones's chest, was also about an inch long but the inspector didn't think this could have been caused by the iron bar. The inspector also found a man's cap with the label inside reading, 'A Barrett & CO, Hatters and Hosiers, Cleveland Terrace, Middlesborough'. Once again Mary Jones and John Carpenter said they had never seen the cap before, which meant that it had belonged to the intruder and that he could have connections with the north-east of England.

The police inspector then sent one of the constables back to the police station to raise the alarm. The Ton Pentre station had recently been fitted with a new private telephone system, which allowed the police, without going through the exchange, to alert all other stations within a twelve-mile radius to be on the lookout for the man, possibly in his stockinged feet. This meant that very quickly police were on the lookout, and a hour later PC David Williams (472) and PC Wood (235) spotted a man coming along the railway line close to the Merlin Hotel on the outskirt of Pontypridd.

The two policemen hid themselves behind the signal box and then as the man approached they jumped out and quickly apprehended him. The police noticed that the man had bloodstains on his face, the back of his head and his coat. He was wearing neither boots nor a hat and in his pockets they found a clam knife and a putty knife which was enough for the police to arrest him on suspicion of murdering John Emlyn Jones. The man gave his name as Eric Lang, said he was a Russian sailor and that he had been born in Riga. The two policemen took him to Pontypridd police station and immediately contacted Inspector Williams at Ton Pentre.

The inspector travelled to Pontypridd, bringing the boots and cap found at the Bridgend Hotel with him. Immediately upon being shown the prisoner, the inspector handed him his boots and the man put them on; they fitted perfectly. So too did the cap.

'Yes, I went there for money,' Lange would later tell Inspector Williams. 'I could not find any in the bar and so I went upstairs and entered the bedroom which was lit up. My mate waited outside while I went in. When I was looking for money she [Mary Jones] woke up and

I hit her with an iron bar. Then he [John Jones] woke up and I struggled with him. I struck him several times with the iron bar and then ran out. My mate Harry must have been behind me.'

Eric Lang as sketched in the *Western Mail*. (*Western Mail*)

The police didn't believe that Eric Lang had an accomplice since Mary Jones said she had only seen one man during the entire struggle with her late husband, and there was no evidence to suggest another man had been present. This mate, this Harry that Lang spoke of, was likely an invention by the prisoner to suggest that it was this man and not himself who had murdered the unfortunate landlord of the Bridgend Hotel.

The inquest on the dead man opened on 12 September when evidence of identification was given. Matters were adjourned until the following day, when a verdict of wilful murder was given. Evidence was presented that Lang had first told police he was a ship's foreman on board the SS *Patria* which was docked in Cardiff, but later he had revealed that was a lie and that he had actually arrived in the area a week or so ago from Liverpool. It was also revealed to the court that when Lang was initially arrested and searched two knives had been found on his person, as well as two handkerchiefs which were heavily bloodstained. The proceedings were again adjourned until 21 September when Lang was finally sent for trial on two charges: burglary and murder.

John Emlyn Jones, the murdered man, in a sketch from the *Western Mail*. (*Western Mail*)

The eventual trial was presided over by Mr Justice Bray on 28 November, with the prosecution led by Mr W.D. Benson and Mr Ivor Bowen, while the defence was handled by Mr Morgan Morgan. The first witness called was Mary Jones and she again recalled the terror of the attack on the morning of 11 September. Despite breaking down into tears at several points in the proceedings, the woman performed well in the witness box and her testimony was followed by that of the cellarman, John Carpenter. Carpenter carefully went through the events of the fateful morning and once he had given evidence he stepped down, and Katie Richards, the niece of Mrs Jones, took the stand. This was the first time she had seen the accused and she revealed that she had seen the man in the public bar a week or two before the murder. This raised the suggestion that Lang had been checking the hotel out, or 'casing' the place, to use criminal parlance. This caused a sensation but other witnesses would reveal that Lang actually had earlier connections to the Bridgend Hotel.

On the second day of the trial Florence Morgan, who had been a barmaid at the Bridgend Hotel for several years, revealed that she knew the man called Lang but when she knew him he had been using a different name. She stated that in the summer of 1901 a foreigner named Eugene Lorenz had come to work at the hotel. He had performed his duties well and there were no complaints about his work, but after a few weeks he had left, stating that 'I don't care for this place.'

To prove she knew the man, Florence described a number of tattoos which she had spotted when Lang/Lorenz had worked at the hotel – a small red and blue star on the back of his left hand, the initials L.O. on his left forearm and an anchor on the back of his right hand. All of these tattoos were found on Eric Lang. The woman then stated that there was a diary at the hotel which would prove what she said.

A day later Inspector Williams gave evidence as to what was in the diary, which referred to a time when the landlord had been a Mr Gould. And entry for Friday, 19 July 1901, read: 'Eugene Lorenz commenced today at 12s per week.' The next entry referring to Lang/Lorenz was dated, Saturday, 27 July and read, 'Eugene Lorenz paid two days, 3s,5d at 12s per week. One week kept in hand.' And then on 24 August an entry read, 'Eugene Lorenz leaving, £1 4s 0d'. This new evidence was further confirmed by Walter Buridge, a drayman who lived at 8 Station Street, Treherbert. In 1901 he too had worked at the hotel and had known the man Eric Lang as Eugene Lorenz.

Inspector Williams was then called back to the stand where he presented evidence to show that the accused had links to Middlesborough. A watch that the accused had been wearing when he was arrested was engraved 'Ligwood and Sons Middlesborough'. The inspector also told the court that investigations revealed that Lang had been known as Eugene Lorenz for more than five years, that he had been born in Riga, had served in the German Navy and that he had arrived in Middlesborough some five years ago when he had married an Irish girl named Bridget Annie Gallagher.

The only witness for the defence was Bridget Lorenz, the wife of the accused, who told the court that her husband had lived with her until he had been paid off for his employment some months back. After that, she claimed, he had started acting funny in the head and then left home. The couple had three children.

Throughout the long trial Lang sat in the box and moaned loudly, several times having to be told to keep quiet. These actions, together with his wife's evidence, may have been intended to give the jury the impression that Lang was suffering from some mental imbalance. For this reason the last witness was Dr Egerton Beggs, the medical officer at Cardiff Prison. He stated that he had examined Lang several times since he had been held there and there had been no signs of any form of insanity. On the contrary, the doctor stated that Lang was 'A calculating man'.

Having heard all the evidence, the jury took just twenty-seven minutes to decide there had been no accomplice named Harry, that

Lang had acted alone and had killed John Emlyn Jones in an attempt to escape the Bridgend Hotel after his bungled robbery. Lang was then sentenced to death.

In the weeks before the execution was carried out, Bridget Lorenz visited her husband as often as she could. All of these meetings took place with an iron grill between them, but shortly before Lang was due to face his sentence she wrote to the prison governor asking for one last meeting without the grill. This was granted and on 20 December, Bridget turned up with her three children for a tearful farewell before Lang finally faced justice.

The press were allowed to attend the execution, which took place in a small shed adjoining 'A' block. The room was lit by a single gaslight which sent shadows around the whitewashed walls as Lang was placed in position over the trap, the executioner, William Billington placed a white cap over Lang's head and the prison chaplain uttered the words, 'I know that my redeemer liveth'. With that the lever was pulled and Lang dropped to his death at precisely 8 am on the morning of Wednesday, 21 December 1904.

Chapter 5

Matricide in Pontycymmer

Pontycymmer is a former mining village situated in the Garw Valley on the outskirts of Bridgend, and it was here in 1907 that thirty-year-old George Stills, a collier, battered his seventy-year-old mother, Rachel Stills, to death.

'Quick,' twelve-year-old, Margaret Leysham called to her older sister. 'Look at this man. He is killing the woman.'

It was around 1.15 on the afternoon of Tuesday 10 September 1907, and the two girls were making their way along Bridgend Road, heading back to school after coming home for dinner, when they heard a loud crash from Number 7. When Margaret peered through the front window, which was on street level, she could see a heavily-built man hitting an elderly woman. The two girls stood in awe, watching the violent scene taking place in the terraced house. What the two girls had witnessed was George Stills, a collier known by the nickname of Knotty because of his muscular physique, beating his elderly mother, Rachel Hannah Stills.

Along the street at Number 11, Mrs Sarah Pryor came outside and noticed the two girls looking through the window. She was joined by another woman, identified in court papers as a Mrs Evans, and the two women watched as the door of Number 7 opened and George Stills emerged. He then shouted at the two inquisitive girls, who were now running down the street, before going back inside, slamming the door closed. Mrs Evans would later tell police that Stills had shouted to the girls, 'If you don't go away from here. I'll give both of you the same.'

Another ten minutes went past and then George Stills came out of the house, carrying his mother in his arms. He laid the old woman down on the pavement and then lifted her skirts up over her face, presumably to hide the fact that she was bloodstained. He then stood there, watching as the two women across the street slowly moved forward. Another women who lived in the street, Ann Davies from Number 17 now came out of her house and together the women went to the aid of Mrs Stills, who lay perfectly still on the pavement.

Seeing the women approaching, Stills went back inside and once again slammed the door behind him. Mrs Stills was still alive, though barely so, and Ann Davies pulled her clothing down for the sake of decency, gasping when she saw the vicious beating the old woman had sustained seemingly at the hands of her own son. Mrs Davies remained with the old women while the other two ran to fetch both a doctor and policeman.

Shortly afterwards, PC Edward Price and Dr John Bowen Jones arrived and found Rachel still lying on the pavement, on her back with her feet towards the house and her head towards the gutter. The policeman knocked on the door and when George Stills answered, he carried the old woman inside and the doctor pronounced her dead. The policeman noted that George Stills had blood on his hands, arms, shirt, trousers and left boot. There was also what appeared to be a fresh wound on his left thumb.

The unfortunate Rachel Hannah Stills. (*Cardiff Times*)

Stills' younger brother, John, then came into the room from the kitchen and told the policeman, 'I have done nothing,' which was confirmed by

George who declared, 'I am the one what done it. I am the man you want.' Stills was then formally cautioned and at around 1.50 pm, Sergeant Charles George Lane and a PC Daniels arrived at the house, having to push past a sizeable crowd that had gathered in the street outside. By this time Rachel's body was laid out in the front room while the doctor completed his examination.

As soon as the sergeant was appraised of the situation he told George Stills that he would be taken to the police station where he would be charged with the murder of his mother.

'I only gave her one blow,' Stills said and was cautioned again, but he persisted in talking, adding: 'I took her outside because I was afraid if I let her in, I would do her further injury.'

Sergeant Lane noticed that there were splashes of blood around the room, and a broken flower pot lay underneath the window. There was a large pool of blood some 2ft from the corner of the front room.

'Not guilty,' George Stills was reported to have said as he was led away to the police station.

That morning George Stills had been in the Ffaldau Arms, a public house which was situated in Oxford Street until it was demolished after a fire in 2007. This was not unusual for George, who often spent mornings drinking heavily and when he made his way home that afternoon he had consumed more than six pints of beer. His mother, during this time, had also been drinking in the Royal Hotel and she too was said to be a little worse for wear when she left to make her way home.

Drink no doubt was a contributing factor in the row between mother and son, an altercation that would end so tragically. George Stills must have been tired, he had gone to the pub straight from a night shift at the local colliery, and not doubt wanted nothing more than to take to his bed, but for some reason that will never be known, he and his mother got into a blazing argument that would end with the mother murdered, and her son facing the death penalty. The Welsh newspapers of the

The Royal Hotel on Bridgend Road, pictured in 2015. The building is now awaiting demolition and it was here that Rachel Stills enjoyed a drink prior to her death. (*Author's collection*)

time reported that there was uproar over the lax licensing laws, which prompted the secretary of the Pontycymmer Constitutional Club to write a letter to the *Glamorgan Gazette*, stating, 'Don't blame us. We turned George Stills down for membership.'

On the morning of 11 September 1907, George Stills appeared before magistrates and was remanded in custody by the stipendiary magistrate, W.J. Lewis. There was a further hearing on 14 September, during which the full details of Mrs Stills' injuries were given to the court by Dr John Bowen Jones.

The woman was dead and had been so for about a quarter of a hour. Her face was covered in blood, and she had been bleeding from the mouth and nose. There was a cut under the chin about two inches long, and down to the bone. There was an irregular cut above her right eyebrow, about an inch and a half in length. This was also down to the bone. There was another cut above the upper lip, about an inch long, through the lips into the mouth.

The left side of the face was swollen and discoloured. There was a cut about three quarters of an inch long on the cheek, and inside the cheek was a wound which went right up in the direction of the eye and back to the angle of the jaw. The lower jaw was fractured on the right side and dislocated on the left.

Once again George Stills was remanded in custody until his full trial at Cardiff Crown Court on 21 November 1907. Mr Justice Sutton presided over the case and the prosecution was led by Mr J. Lloyd Morgan, while Mr B. Francis Williams staged the defence. Stills admitted killing his mother, but claimed there had been no intent to do so. His defence were to argue that he was guilty of manslaughter rather than the capital offence of murder.

In his opening speech, Mr J. Lloyd Morgan told the court that during the morning before Rachel met her death, her husband (also George Stills) and both of her sons had been drinking at the Ffaldau Hotel. John Stills was the first to leave, saying that he was going home to bed. It was only ten minutes or so later that George himself left leaving his father on his own in the Hotel. It was stated that although George had been drinking, he was not drunk, which was confirmed by a friend, Thomas Jones of Number 6 Greenhill, Pontycymmer, who told the court he saw George come out of the hotel. The two men passed the time of day and Jones, in his police statement, said George was not staggering or unsteady on his feet and seemed to be in an excellent mood.

Various neighbours where then called to give evidence and afterwards the court was adjourned for the day. The case had generated so much newspaper coverage, matricide being such a rare crime, that a sensation was caused on the second day of the trial when noted actor,

Sir Herbert Beerbohm Tree, the actor Oliver Reed's grandfather, who was appearing in Cardiff's New Theatre, turned up and sat in the pubic gallery.

The actor Sir Herbert Beerbohm Tree. (*Commons source file*)

The defence argued that Rachel Stills had herself been drunk on the day of her death, and that she had, whilst in a state of drunkenness, provoked her son. However, a neighbour, Mrs Sarah Pryor testified that she had seen Mrs Stills at 7.30 am and that she was certainly not drunk then. The woman also refuted the claims of the defence that Mrs Stills was quite drunk and another neighbour, Margaret Ann Stone, told the court that although she had often seen Mrs Stills the worse for wear due to drink, she had spoken to her on that fateful morning and she was certainly sober. Dr Edward Parry then took to the witness box and stated that he had known Mrs Stills for a number of years, and though he had often seen her 'merry', he had never seen her drunk. Evidence was given that Mrs Stills had been in the Royal Hotel in the hours prior to her death, but the landlord said she had certainly not been drunk when she had left.

The defence then called George Stills senior, the prisoner's father, who told the court that he had been married to Mrs Stills for forty-six years, and that during the last twenty she had been more a beast than a woman. He told the court that his wife drank heavily and this meant that the house was not a happy one. He went onto say that if anyone said the wrong thing to his wife she would go into a violent temper and had many times struck him or his sons with a jug or a bottle. He claimed that she had more than once brandished a knife in his face and threatened to slit his throat open.

In the closing speech, the defence told the jury that there was no question that George Stills had taken his mother's life, but that he had acted after such extreme provocation as to reduce the crime to manslaughter. The defence reminded the jury that witnesses had testified that George Stills had been in a good frame of mind when he'd left his father in the hotel on that fateful morning. The prosecution refuted

George Stills. (*Western Mail*)

this, telling the jury that they could not simply assume that such provocation took place and that the correct verdict should be murder. It took the jury just six minutes to bring in a verdict of wilful murder, and the judge then put on the black cap and passed the death sentence.

On Friday, 13 December 1907, Stills woke early in Cardiff prison and partook of a light breakfast, followed by three cigarettes. His was visited in his cell by the Reverend H.H. Adams who reported that the prisoner's final words to him were, 'Tell my old comrades to stay away from the drink, and to take advantage of all opportunities that come their way.' The prisoner than recited the verse, God be with you until we meet again. Reverend Adams stated that George Stills met his maker with courage and the conviction that everlasting salvation awaited him.

At 8 am, he was led to the scaffold by Henry and Thomas Pierrepoint where he met his doom. Outside the prison, several hundred people waited for the notice of execution to be posted.

Chapter 6

Madness and Manslaughter

'**D**one to Death with an Umbrella,' was the sensational headline carried by the *Rhondda Leader* newspaper on 17 February 1906. The story which followed told of 43-year-old, Robert Lloyd from Treherbert, who during a drunken argument with another man, had died after being struck in the eye with an umbrella, an argument that had started over the toss of a coin.

It had started off like any other Saturday night in the Railway Hotel, which was situated in Treherbert at the head of the Rhondda Valley. As usual, the public bar was packed and it was here that Robert Lloyd, a labourer from the village, went for a few

Robert Lloyd. (*Cardiff Times*)

drinks with friends. It was 10 February 1906. A bitter and biting wind howled through the valley but there was a warm glow inside the bar and the patrons were oblivious to the bluster outside.

William and James Phillips, with another man David Evans, known locally as Dai Bach, were sat across the bar from Robert Lloyd. And the three men were tossing coins to decide who would buy the next round of drinks when an argument broke out. During the argument, James Phillips pushed Dai Bach, a much smaller man, from his stool. Robert Lloyd witnessed this and being good friends with Dai Bach it angered him, particularly as Phillips was a much bigger man. He went across to the three men had had words, specifically calling James Phillips a coward for picking on a much smaller man.

'Why don't you pick on someone your own size?' Robert Lloyd was reported to have said.

Phillips and Lloyd then went toe to toe and blows were exchanged before the landlord came across and ordered the two men out of the pub. William Phillips then got involved and told his brother, James to calm down. The two brothers then left the public bar with Robert Lloyd, their argument seemingly forgotten. Outside though the argument started afresh, with Robert Lloyd telling Phillips that he should apologise to Dai Bach. Once again the men went toe to toe, and seconds later Robert Lloyd lay on the hard pavement, dead. No one seemed to know exactly what had happened and witness reports conflicted, although all seemed to agree that no actual blows had been traded.

Charles Culverhouse, a friend of Lloyd who witnessed the argument, said he had heard a whizzing sound and then saw something, he wasn't sure what, strike Lloyd in the corner of the head. After that Robert Lloyd had immediately fallen backwards and onto the ground. He was bleeding profusely from his forehead, nose and mouth and, gruesomely, his right eye was out and hung on his cheek. He lay there, without uttering a sound and bled to death.

Shocked bystanders, not realizing the extent of Lloyd's injuries, lifted up the man but could get no response from him. They carried him to his home, which was nearby in Taff Street. His wife called in the local doctor, who pronounced Robert Lloyd dead. PC David Davies, the first officer to arrive at the home of Robert Lloyd, later stated. 'I visited 16 Taff Street, Treherbert. On the sofa in the back parlour I saw the body of the deceased, Robert Lloyd. I examined him and found a jagged wound about three quarters of an inch and reaching from his eyebrow to the corner of his right eye, gaping very much and blood running from it [*sic*]. The skull was fractured and the right eye discoloured. His shirt was saturated with blood; his coat was off.'

After talking to several witnesses, the police felt they had gathered enough evidence to arrest both of the Phillips brothers and charge them jointly with murdering Robert Lloyd. It had been discovered that it had been an umbrella that had struck Robert Lloyd in the side of the head, the umbrella that James Phillips habitually carried. The police found the umbrella in Jason Phillips's home and noticed that the ferrule was missing from the end.

The following Monday, the inquest took place at Treherbert police station. Coroner R.J. Rees presided and the solicitor for the defence was a Mr T. Millward of Tonypandy. It was at the inquest that Dr D.C. Williams gave sensational evidence regarding to the post-mortem examination he had performed on the unfortunate Robert Lloyd. The doctor had removed the top of the man's skull and found the brain to be in a healthy condition. Upon removing a triangular bone above the injured eye, he observed a quantity of fluid mixed with blood. There was a fracture to the spheroid bone and when closely examining the wound around the bone, the doctor had pulled an umbrella ferrule and a washer from the wound. The cause of death was shock and haemorrhage. The coroner asked the doctor if sufficient force would be required to drive an umbrella into a man's head, leaving the ferrule behind. The doctor said he felt that this would be the case.

A statement that James Phillips had made to the police at the time of his arrest was then read out: 'I had a row with a fellow in the bar who was sitting on a stool. I upset him and Bob Lloyd got in a bad way with me. I told him I would not fight him in the bar, so we went outside to the road. "Come on with me, or I will do you with this umbrella," I said. I don't know, but I suppose he must have fallen against it.'

An eyewitness backed up what James and said, and the witness claimed that although he saw James Phillips holding up his umbrella, pointing it at Robert Lloyd, he could not say if the umbrella had struck the man or not. The witness agreed that it was certainly possible that Lloyd had fallen against the umbrella, thus driving it into his own head. This contradicted an earlier witnesses statement given to police, when Charles Culverhouse had said that Robert Lloyd had fallen backwards after being struck on the side of the head.

A month later James Phillips stood trial for manslaughter at the Glamorgan Assizes in Cardiff. The prosecution was led by Lloyd Morgan MP, while a Mr Ivor Bowen appeared for the defence. There seemed to be strong evidence against Phillips, with several witnesses stating that it had been James Phillips who had delivered the fatal blow with the umbrella, and Dr Williams even brought a model skull into the court and demonstrated how the fatal injuries had been delivered.

The defence then delivered its case. Much was made of the fact that James Phillips had been employed in America, and had contacted blood poisoning after working in a flooded mine, and had ever since had to carry the umbrella to aid in his walking. The court was told that Phillips found it embarrassing to use a walking stick and thus the umbrella served as a substitute. The defence also sketch out the long-lasting friendship between the accused and the dead man. How could he have harmed Robert Lloyd, the jury were asked, when the two men were such good friends and the accused didn't have the physical ability to do so.

The jury took only a minute to come to the verdict of 'Not Guilty'. The unfortunate affair had been, they decided, a tragic accident. James Phillips would walk from the court a free man, but not before the judge told him, 'You have, unfortunately under circumstances which were accidental, caused the death of a man who had been your friend. I hope this serves as a warning to you to keep away from the drink.'

The Tragic Love Triangle

Domestic arguments are all too common, though where most culminate in apologies and conciliatory kisses, there are times when the end result can be devastating. Such devastation was caused in October 1906.

Margaret Jones lived a complicated life. She was married but separated from her husband John, who lived in Treorchy whilst Margaret had most recently lived in Newport. Until a few months previously, Margaret had resided at 7 Morgan Terrace, Porth with her lover George Phillips, a collier. She had been with Phillips for a little over five years before leaving him for another man, Harry Scratton and moving to Newport. In fact it had been George Phillips whom Margaret had left her husband to be with, but when their relationship soured she set her eyes on another man. Harry Scratton, a labourer, was a friend of Phillips and it was this friendship that first brought him together with Margaret. Scratton became a regular visitor at the house in Porth and soon started an affair with Margaret with culminated in her leaving her lover, George Phillips and fleeing to Newport with Scratton.

A month after moving to Newport, Margaret found herself back in the valleys when she took a job as a chambermaid at Pontypridd's New Inn. Finding herself in close proximity to her former lover Margaret realized, after Phillips contacted her several times, that he was hoping for a reconciliation, that they could put this business with Scratton behind them. Margaret though, was still very much with Scratton and would commute by train between Pontypridd and Newport.

On the night of 20 October 1906 Margaret and Scratton decided on a night out in the valleys. The plan was for Margaret to meet Scratton in Treherbert when she finished work. At around 6.15 that evening, Margaret boarded the train at Pontypridd and was dismayed to find that George Phillips was following her. During the

Margaret Jones. (*Cardiff Times*)

journey Phillips sat several seats behind Margaret. He didn't speak to her, nor acknowledge her at all but Margaret could feel his eyes on her.

When the train pulled into Ystrad station, Margaret got off in order to escape Phillips, but once again he followed her. There was a policeman on the platform and Margaret approached him, informing the officer that George Phillips was following her. The policeman had words with George Phillips, ordering him to return home, while Margaret jumped on the next train that would take her to Treherbert.

Later that night Margaret and Scratton boarded the 9 pm train from Treherbert that would bring them back down the valleys and onto Cardiff, where they would be able to take another train to their home in Newport. But when the train pulled into Porth station, George Phillips got on and entered the carriage where Margaret and Scratton were sitting. There were two other people in the carriage, later identified as Miss John, a woman from Trehafod and a Mr Francis Gear of North Street, Porth. These two innocents would become witnesses to the terrible events that were about to unfold.

Phillips immediately approached the couple at the rear of the carriage and a blazing argument started. This resulted in Phillips and Scratton trading blows as the train moved at full speed towards Trehafod. Phillips quickly bested Scratton, a much smaller man, and delivered a stinging punch that sent him sprawling to the floor. Margaret then intervened, getting up and pushing Phillips away from the downed man, but Phillips didn't so much as stagger before turning on the woman. He delivered a series of brutal blows to her head and face. Margaret staggered backwards against the carriage door. Margaret then opened the door and either fell or jumped out. Witnesses couldn't be sure on this point.

'She's gone out the door,' Phillips shouted at the dazed Scratton. 'Bloody go after her.'

Scratton, however, started to fight back and the two men resumed trading blows as the train continued on its way. The two men were still fighting when the train pulled into Trehafod station where Mr Gear quickly got off and told the station master what was happening. The police were called and a PC Lucus, from Pontypridd, attended and quickly arrested George Phillips and Harry Scratton. It was only when the situation calmed down somewhat that it was decided to find out what had happened to Margaret.

It was discovered that Margaret had, when jumping or falling from the train, been struck by a mineral train passing alongside. William Brad, the driver was shunting on the line between Trehafod and Porth when he felt a slight jerk. He had immediately stopped the train and gone to see what had caused this and come across the cruelly injured woman. She was barely alive, both of her legs and one arm having been severed from her body. A doctor attended to the woman, finding her in a pitiful state. And an ambulance was quickly arranged and she was taken to Cardiff Royal Infirmary.

George Phillips was taken to Porth police station and charged with causing grievous bodily harm to Margaret Jones. Scratton had been released without charge and had made his way to the infirmary to be with the hideously injured woman. However, several hours later Margaret Jones died of her injuries, perhaps mercifully so.

The following day, George Phillips had his charge altered to the much more serious one of causing the death of the woman. The later inquest returned a verdict of unlawful killing and Phillips was committed for a full trial. As the coroner was sure Phillips hadn't physically pushed Margaret from the train, bail was granted while the court case was pending.

On 23 November of that year, George Phillips stood before the Glamorgan Assizes, with the case presided over by a Mr Justice Wotton. Witnesses were called and once again no one seemed sure if Margaret had fallen from the train, or had jumped out. Much was made of the fact that the five-year relationship between George Phillips and the deceased had been turbulent, witnesses stating that Phillips was often cruel to the woman. It was said that because of this cruelty the relationship between the deceased and Harry Scratton had initially developed. George Phillips would be found guilty of manslaughter and sentenced to six months hard labour.

Between Brothers

Williamstown is a small village in the Rhondda Valley. Founded in 1870, and located at the foot of *Mynydd Dinas*, it is today, like many of the former mining villages, a peaceful place to live. The industrial scars that once speckled the mountains have now disappeared, replaced by lush greenery but there is one scar that the tiny village still carries, and even today it is an open wound for some. The story has been passed down from generation to generation, and people still talk in hushed tones of the tragic event that befell the village in 1909.

On the evening of 21 April, Mrs Baker had stood on the doorstep of her home on Penygraig Road and watched the two brothers arguing at the end of the road. She knew the boys as Sydney and George Young, two brothers, who lived locally and came from a good family. She watched as Sydney, the younger of two boys, ran off and then she witnessed George collapsing to the ground. She would later say that she had heard him groan slightly as he fell.

Mrs Baker was then joined by another local woman, a Mrs Adams, and together the women went to assist George Young. They were shocked to find blood oozing from a small wound in his chest. They tried to assist him, lifting to head to speak to him but his condition quickly worsened and he fell unconscious. The women called a couple of men from nearby houses and they carried the boy to his home at 8 Brook Street, and his anxious parents immediately sent for a doctor. The boy though would die before the arrival of medical help. George Young was just sixteen years old, and his brother, Sydney, who had presumably caused the fatal wound, was a year younger.

Number 8 Brook Street, Williamstown, as it looks today. It was here that George Young succumbed to his injuries. (*Author's collection*)

Prior to the incident on Penygraig Road, Sydney Young had been with a group of youths at the corner of Brook Street, when his brother, George came upon him. The elder brother, feeling that his sibling was in bad company, told him to go home and an argument broke out between the two.

'If you don't leave me alone I will run this through you,' Sydney was reported to have said, holding a small pocket knife.

There was a scuffle between the brothers and Sydney soon ran off with George going after him. This would culminate in the boys having their fatal argument at the corner of Penygraig Road. The argument had started out over nothing of much account, and yet the consequences were dire and tore the family apart. The brothers reportedly had a good relationship, with George being the more reserved of the two, while Sydney could be rambunctious at times. Both boys were employed as collier boys at the Cambrian Colliery at nearby Clydach Vale.

The police were soon called to Brook Street and an Inspector Hole arrived from Tonypandy. He, together with a Sergeant Thomas, arranged for a search to find Sydney Young and his description was sent to neighbouring police stations. A police cordon was quickly set up around the area, but even so it was not until midnight that the boy was found. He had been discovered close to the Ely Pits and immediately arrested and taken to Tonypandy police station. He was promptly charged with the capital offence of wilful murder, which caused the most harrowing grief for his parents who had not only lost one of their children, but had to accept the reality that the loss had been caused by the actions of their second child.

'I didn't mean it,' a tearful Sydney told police. 'I held out the knife and George rushed at me, falling on the blade.'

The knife used in the attack was never recovered and Sydney told the police that he couldn't remember what he had done with it. He thought that he had thrown it somewhere when the awful realisation of what had happened truly dawned on him.

The resulting trial was a sensation and crowds gathered outside the Ton Pentre juvenile court, but it was decided that only those directly involved would be allowed into such sensitive proceedings. The court would hear that it had been George who had been the aggressor and started the argument that would end so tragically. He had come upon his younger brother, who together with two other boys had been talking to a couple of girls, and promptly ordered him home. Sydney had taken umbrage at this and refused, and it was then that George pushed him and a scuffle broke out.

David Jones, a fifteen-year-old who had been one of the boys with Sydney, told the court that George had thrown stones at them before the fight started. He said that Sydney had threatened George with the knife, but that the older brother had fallen onto the blade. Sydney would stand in the dock throughout the court case, his head bowed and his shoulders shaking as he openly sobbed.

Before a verdict was reached, papers were brought before the court that outlined a new Act of Parliament. The change in the law meant that were Sydney found guilty of wilful murder, he would not face the death penalty, since that minors would no longer be executed if found guilty of capital murder. Sydney Young had the distinction of being the first person tried under this new law.

Sydney Young escaped a murder conviction, however, the jury returning a verdict of manslaughter, with a recommendation of mercy given the youth of the accused and the suffering he and his family had already endured. It was concluded by the court that the argument between the two brothers had been nothing more than an everyday argument and that in ninety-nine out of a hundred cases, George would have likely only received a flesh wound from the knife used. It was the most unfortunate bad luck that the wound had proved fatal.

The judge, in summing up, told the court that he felt although the boy was technically guilty of manslaughter, he had not meant his brother any real harm and that he had killed him by accident. The judge also felt that George had been the aggressor and that no real culpability could be attached to Sydney. He saw no justification for sending the boy to prison and instead bound the boy over until a full trial. Sydney Young faced that judgement at Swansea Assizes, on 21 July, when he pleaded guilty to manslaughter. Mr Justice Stratton heard the case and agreed that the killing had been largely accidental and he set the boy free, but warned him that he might in the future face further judgement.

Sydney Young would not appear in court again, but he was left deeply scarred by the knowledge that he had killed his own brother.

Chapter 7

The Confession

'Murder. I have thrown Sloppy down a hole in the old works. She told me she was going to give me away for living on her prostitution and I done for the bugger.'

The two policemen, Sergeant Charles Hunter and PC Richard Lewis, stopped in their tracks. When they'd started patrolling the streets of Merthyr Tydfil on a particularly cold December night in 1908, they certainly hadn't expected this. And yet here before them stood a man, who had identified himself as William Foy, demanding to be locked up for murder.

'If you come with me, I will show you where she is,' Foy continued.

At that point Hunter cautioned Foy and then the two policemen allowed him to lead them down to Castle Street to locate his claimed victim. During the walk, Foy pulled 10d out of his pockets and handed it to the sergeant, asking the policeman to give it to his sister. It was then that they were joined by Detective Constable Edward Jones who had come out of a house at the end of the street. The detective was informed of the situation and then joined the men as Foy took them towards the old Ynysfach Ironworks.

'I will swing for the bugger,' the talkative Foy predicted.

The four men arrived at the Ynysfach Ironworks, where there were several disused coke ovens. The ironworks had been built in 1801 by the industrialist Thomas Jones and initially consisted of two furnaces, both steam-powered, and an engine house. In 1830 two more furnaces were added as well as another engine house but by 1909 the ironworks were falling into ruin after being closed in 1884.

'This is where I threw the bugger down,' Foy told the police, pointing to a plank of wood which lay across and old coal bunker. 'She won't worry me no more.' Sergeant Hunter led Foy across the plank and shone his torch down into the depths of the furnace, but he could see nothing. The other policemen joined them and also shone their torches down into the blackness but there was no body to be seen.

'I caught hold of her there,' Foy pointed to some marks on the ground. 'I swung her round and dropped her down the hole. I will get a bucket of fire to drop in if you can't see the bugger.'

By now the police were considering the possibility that Foy was leading them a merry dance, but he led them to a second oven where there was indeed a fire burning in a small bucket. There was also a man and a woman laying on the ground next to the fire and they sat up when Foy entered with the three policemen. The man was John Edward Bassett and the woman gave her name as Mary Greaney.

When asked about the woman Foy referred to as Sloppy, actually Mary Ann Rees, a local woman known as a prostitute, Bassett told

Ynysfach Ironworks as painted by Penry Williams in 1819. (*The National Museum of Wales*)

the police that Foy had already told them that he had killed the woman, but they didn't believe him. He was the worse for drink and they wouldn't put it past Foy to make up such a wild story. He was, Bassett concluded, 'A right Tom Pepper' – Tom Pepper, of course, being a mythical character who was kicked out of Hell for his preposterous lies.

The police decided to escort Foy back to the police station and deposit him in a cell, before returning to the old ironworks with a rope. A lamp was tied to the end of the rope and lowered into the gaping maw of the old furnace and sure enough the body of Mary Ann Rees was discovered.

To recover the body the police had to enter the furnace through a culvert at ground level, the furnace being almost 40ft deep. A doctor arrived to officially pronounce death and then the unfortunate Mary Ann Rees was taken by cart to the doctor's surgery for a detailed examination. At 5.00 am on Christmas Eve, 1909, two doctors, Dr John Chilsholm and Dr Ward, made the examination. The woman's face was very badly bruised, the skin ripped across the right cheek, the upper jaw was fractured and there was extensive haematoma of the right eye. There were abrasions on both arms, the chest, abdomen, thighs and legs. The later post-mortem would reveal the abdomen was full of blood, the result of the right renal vein being severed. The right kidney was loose and it was concluded that the injuries were consistent with the woman having being thrown into the furnace.

At 9 pm that night William Joseph Foy was charged with murder and made a brief appearance before magistrates where the case was adjourned, with Foy remanded in custody. On 28 December the inquest returned a verdict of unlawful killing, as did the magistrates court the following day and Foy was duly sent for trial.

On the last day of March 1909, Foy found himself facing the Cardiff Assizes with Mr Justice Bray hearing the case. The prosecution was led by Mr W. Llewellyn Williams, while Mr Ivor Bowen appeared for the defence. It seemed that it was going to be a straightforward case with Foy's confession being the main thrust of the prosecution's case.

The first witness was convicted prostitute Mary Greaney, who had been at the ironworks with John Bassett on the night that Mary Ann, or Sloppy as she was commonly known, met her death. The woman told the court that she had been released from prison on the morning of 23 December 1908 and that Sloppy had been outside the prison gates to meet her. They caught a train to Merthyr Tydfil and went to the Wheatsheaf public house for a celebratory drink. They then went onto the Rainbow Inn where they once again had a drink. Afterwards they bought some food and then went up to the Ynysfach Works, where Foy and John Bassett where waiting for them. The disused ironworks was a popular spot for prostitutes to ply their trade and the meeting had been pre-arranged. When asked what time this was, the woman told the court that this was about 11 am.

All four of them ate together and then went back down to the town where Sloppy went off with a man, receiving a shilling for her favours. Later that evening they all met up again in the Red Lion pub, where drinks where consumed and then it was Mary Greaney's turn to go off and service a client. At around 10.30 that night all four again met in the Rainbow Inn where even more drinks were consumed before they all went off to the old ironworks where it would be cosy.

'It is Polly Gough you want!' Sloppy was reported to have yelled, pushing Foy in the chest as she spoke.

It was around midnight when Sloppy put on her shoes and stormed off into the night. Foy went after her. Shortly afterwards Foy came back into the disused coke oven where Bassett and Mary Greaney were sat around a small fire. He told the two that he had tossed Sloppy into a hole but neither of them believed him.

John Bassett, describing himself a labourer, next took the stand and confirmed the evidence given by Mary Greaney. He added that he and Foy regularly slept in the old coke ovens and that the women knew this. The various police officers involved in the case where then called to give their evidence and finally Foy was called to the stand himself.

It was now that Foy changed his story, claiming that Sloppy had fallen into the hole, that it had all been a terrible accident. The defence now questioned Foy, asking why he had made his original statements that he had thrown the woman into the hole and he replied that he had been in deep shock at the time. He considered himself responsible for Mary Ann's death but had not caused it deliberately. They had struggled and she had fallen down the hole.

The jury, however, believed Foy's original statements and found him guilty of murder and he was sentenced to death. The execution was originally to have been carried out on 20 April, but this was postponed when Foy appealed against his conviction. The appeal was heard by Justices Darling, Lawrence and Bray but was unsuccessful and Foy was led back into custody to await his appointment with the hangman.

On a fine Saturday in May of that year. William Joseph Foy woke to a fine breakfast of beefsteak before walking to the gallows at Swansea Prison. He was hanged by Henry Pierrepoint and John Ellis, his final words were reported to have been, 'Show mercy Lord.'

Chapter 8

Infanticide and Child Murders

A ll murders are equally terrible, and yet the murder of a child or infant is all the more emotive. Very often the victims are helpless, unable to defend themselves and quite often the perpetrator is someone trusted by the child – a parent, family member or legal guardian. Infanticide is defined in the 1938 Infanticide Act as the killing of a child below twelve months of age and these particular crimes provoke revulsion and anger in society but this wasn't always the case. In Victorian Britain child killings often went unreported, with the authorities torn between legal patriarchy and the sanctity of family life. Among the ruling classes, there was a general apathy and detachment towards working-class children, which was reflected in the fact that few cases of sudden child death ever saw the inside of a courtroom.

But it wasn't always murder or manslaughter that ended a child's life. Heartbreaking neglect was a common cause of child death in the nineteenth and early twentieth centuries. Infanticide in particular would often be written off as a stillbirth because there was precious little way of proving otherwise. And a put-upon mother living in hopeless poverty, suddenly finding herself with another mouth to feed, might see no option other than ridding herself of her new child. A direct result of the 1834 Poor Law Amendment Act, which saw a reduction in the help given to unmarried mothers, saw many babies abandoned outside churches and chapels . Though it wasn't only crime that could end a child's life and history is full of cases where genuine accidents brought about tragic consequences. There were instances of children dying from drinking whisky or carbolic acid left around the house, or burning to death as the result of an unattended candle or open fire, and outside the home children would have fatal accidents whilst playing close to industrial machinery or run over by carts. It wasn't until well into the twentieth century that the NSPCC and other reformers took the initiative and pushed for changes in the law, which protected children from the neglect and violence that blighted not only their own lives but the communities within which they lived.

The following chapter details just several cases of a large number that are held in police records.

Infanticide

One of the earliest recorded cases of infanticide in South Wales was an 1886 case when in May of that year, thirty-year-old Helen Stokes found herself before magistrates after the death of her new-born baby. Mrs Stokes was married to a soldier, Thomas Stokes, but he had been away from home for more than three years and was currently serving in India. The court was told that in all the time he had been away Mrs Stokes had only received the sum of £2 to help in raising their six-year-old son.

It was on the morning of Wednesday, 19 May that Mrs Stokes was visited by her mother-in-law who was worried because the woman hadn't been seen for several days. Mrs Stokes was in bed and told her mother-in-law that she was not well, and would not be getting up that day. It was then that the elder woman peered under the bed and saw the dead body of a new-born baby. This was a shock, more so because no one had had any idea that Helen Stokes had been pregnant. There was also the fact that her husband was away serving in the military and had not been home for several years, the child could not have been his.

The police were called and an Inspector Jones arrived from Porth who noted that Mrs Stokes seemed nonplussed at the passing of her baby. The policeman immediately sent for a doctor and Dr Davies arrived and pronounced the baby dead, he also commented that Mrs Stokes appeared to be in a state of deep depression. An eventual post-mortem was carried out on the baby, a boy, and it was discovered that he had not been stillborn but had died because his mother had failed to attend to his needs. All the evidence suggested that as soon as she had given birth, Mrs Stokes had placed the infant beneath her bed and ignored it.

The coroner's inquest was held on 21 May at the Vaughn Arms and Helen Stokes was later found guilty of manslaughter for her failure to care for the new-born child. The community felt considerable sympathy for the woman, events such as this were commonplace. During this period it was a hard existence for the working classes and even more so for a woman trying to raise children on her own.

Eight years later the Rhondda Valley would again be shocked when Margaret Jenkins of Tynewydd, was brought before the courts on charges of murdering her own baby. This case was all the more alarming, since Mrs Jenkins had decapitated her infant daughter with an axe.

It was 8 May 1894 when David Jenkins was awoken by his wife calling him from downstairs. Jenkins had worked the night shift and he was tired as he pulled himself from bed, and made his way downstairs to see what the problem was.

'*Rwy wedi cwpa babi*,' Margaret, speaking in Welsh, told her husband as he came into the sitting room and found her sitting in an armchair before the fire. What she had said was: 'I have finished the baby off.' And when David asked where their daughter was his wife pointed to the pantry.

The sight that met David Jenkins when he went into the pantry was terrible beyond imagination. There on the salting table was the headless corpse of their infant daughter, Elizabeth Anne. Her head was on the floor, a bloodied axe beside it. Jenkins was left dazed by the discovery and he immediately left the house, returning a while later with a policeman, PC T. Bryan of Treherbert. The policeman wrapped the baby up in a napkin and then arrested Margaret Jenkins, charging her with the wilful murder of her child.

'Yes, I did it with the axe,' she was reported to have replied.

Post-natal depression was not recognized at this time, but much was made during the trial of the woman's mental state. Indeed when Dr Llewllyn Powell took to the witness box he stated that, 'I should be disposed to believe that during childbirth puerperal mania can develop. In these cases people can get very cruel, and are known to attack those that they are most fond of.'

On Wednesday, 27 June 1884, Margaret Jenkins was found guilty of feloniously and with malice aforethought killing her daughter on 18 May 1884. Facing a murder charge, there was a very real possibility that Margaret would stand before the hangman, but in the end the jury returned a verdict that the woman was unfit to plead due to insanity. She was sentenced to be detained at Her Majesty's Pleasure.

In 1916, with the news full of the horrors of the Great War, there was an incident in the Rhondda Valley that temporarily pushed the details of battles fought on some foreign battlefield from the front pages. 'Ystrad Sensation!', screamed the *Rhondda Herald*, 'Rhondda Horror,' reported the *South Wales Echo*.

It was in March of that year that Councillor Thomas James of Penrhys Road decided to see what he could do about a blocked drain at the rear of his house. The weather had been very wet recently and his back yard was starting to flood. He poked a long stick into the drain, feeling a blockage and teasing it out. He was horrified to discover the source of the blockage; there in the filthy water floated the head of an infant baby. The police were promptly summoned and a PC Storehouse made the grim discovery of the baby's torso and legs in the main drain. The poor child's arms were never found.

An inquest was held and post-mortem evidence stated that the child had been dead for about two days. The jury were told that the parents of the baby were unknown as of the present time and it was up to them to decide whether this was a case of murder or the minor crime of concealment of a birth. The coroner, a Mr R.J. Rees stated, with bizarre logic: 'In my opinion murder is not an option as there would seem little reason to sever the head and arms. It seems to be simply a matter of a child dying due to lack of attention at birth, and its body being mutilated to aid concealment.'

It took just one hour for the jury to return an open verdict and the case was closed with the parents of the child never being found. This sums up the general attitude of the time; there was little time or effort made to trace the child's parents and the case was quickly forgotten, with the child being buried in a pauper's grave. To the modern mind this is astounding, yet at the time the lack of interest by the authorities was not unusual. This unfortunate child had merely been just another part of the grim realities of working-class life.

The Baby Farmer

In August 1907 Rhoda Willis marked her forty-fourth birthday by becoming the first and only woman to be hanged at Cardiff Prison. A dubious honour indeed, but history also records her as the last woman to be hanged in Wales, and the last baby farmer to hanged anywhere in the United Kingdom. By all accounts she showed great fortitude and remained calm as Henry and Thomas Pierrepoint led her to the scaffold.

A few months earlier she had been going by the name of Leslie James and was employed as a live in housekeeper at 55 George Street in Pontypool. Her employer was David Evans, a cobbler who was estranged from his wife and had decided to employ Rhoda after finding that single-handedly managing both a business and home was too much for him. With someone to take care of domestic duties for he would be free to pursue his business interests. The woman he knew as Leslie James was an extremely attractive woman, with large expressive eyes and thick auburn hair, and the two became very close. Eventually they would become lovers but for the sake of propriety they kept their dalliance secret. To the outside world the relationship was that of employer and employee.

The truth about Rhoda Willis was that she had been born Rhoda Leselles in Sunderland on 14 August 1863, and had taken the name Willis when at the tender age of nineteen years, she had married a marine engineer named Thomas Willis. They had set up the marital home in Grangetown, Cardiff and by all accounts lived happily with a daughter blessing their union. That happiness though was to be shattered in 1895, when George Thomas fell in and died. Rhoda then met another marine engineer named Leslie James and they set up home together, though they were never married. In time the relationship developed and they had two children before problems arose and they separated.

For a while Rhoda brought up her children alone, but she found this increasingly difficult. The result of this was that she left the children with relatives and adopted the name of Leslie James, done so she claimed so as not to bring shame on her family, and moved onto Pontypool. This was where she met David Evans and started along the road that would lead her to the hangman. Rhoda decided early in March of 1907 that she needed to earn extra revenue and by using her feminine wiles on David Evans, she was able to persuade him to allow her to take in a child for a financial consideration. No doubt Evans was dubious about this but the woman was able to perfectly manipulate him and he agreed to the idea.

It was on 20 March of that year that the following advertisement appeared in the 'Miscellaneous Wants' section of the *Evening Express*:

Married couple – Christian people, good position, wish to adopt baby entirely as own; every comfort and care; must be healthy; small premium – apply E44.

Two replies were eventually received, the first from Emily Stroud of Abertillery and the second from Lydia English of Fleur-de-lis, near Hengoed. Rhoda replied to both women and soon heard back from Lydia English who explained that her unmarried sister was to deliver a child around May. A second latter then came; this time from Emily Stroud who had already given birth, delivering a healthy boy.

Rhoda wrote back to the woman, saying that she would be delighted to take in the baby and a one off premium of £6 was suggested. Several letters went back and forth until on 10 April, Rhonda travelled to Abertillery and took charge of the baby boy. For this the mother paid £6 and after a tearful farewell she walked away from a baby she would never see again. Shortly afterwards, Rhoda wrote to Lydia English, stating that she had now taken in a baby and would be unable to assist when her sister gave birth. Mrs English, however, was not easily put off and she requested she visit so that the two of them could talk. A week later Lydia English came to see Rhoda at the home of David Evans.

The two women spent an entire afternoon talking and once Lydia English had returned home, Rhoda informed David Evans that Mrs English was in desperate need of someone to adopt the baby, and had offered them £5 to do so. This time, though, Evans was not to be persuaded and he told Rhoda to forget it and concentrate on the child they already had. At first Rhoda seemed to agree with Evans but then she received another letter, this time from a Mr Stanley Rees. In his letter the man explained that he was a married man and that his wife had recently given birth to a baby. They were happy but he was about to take on a new business venture which would necessitate them moving abroad. They could not take the baby with them and were seeking someone to provide the child with a good home. The sum of £10 was mentioned, to be paid in two £5 instalments. Rhoda was not going to let this considerable sum of money escape her, and she began to think of options open to her. She would take the second child, but the problem was this meant she would have to rid herself of the child she already had.

It must have played on the woman's mind but she formulated a plan and in early May, Rhoda informed David Evans that she was to receive an inheritance of £320, an absolute fortune during the time, and that she would have to travel to Birmingham. She said that she would leave the baby in the care of a friend in Llanishen, Cardiff while she was away.

And so it was that on 7 May at 10.15 pm, Major Emma Chatterton of the Salvation Army noticed a small bundle outside her home at Charles Street, Cardiff. Upon examination the bundle was found to contain a baby. The child was securely wrapped in red flannel to which a note was pinned. The note read:

Dear Kaptain do take my baby in, I am won of your girls but gon rong I will come back if you fergie me I bring sum muny [*sic*].

Rhoda was an educated woman and the note's misspellings and grammatical mistakes were a ploy to hide this fact, but with this simple act of child abandonment Rhoda Willis had become a baby farmer.

The term baby farming was used in late Victorian Britain to mean the act of taking in a child for payment; this often involved wet nursing (breast feeding of a child by someone other than the natural mother). Some baby farmers adopted the children for a fee, while others cared for children for periodic payments. In the years before adoption and fostering were regulated by the state, baby farmers offered a way for unmarried women to escape the stigma of illegitimate child birth. These were harsh and overly pious times and the birth of an illegitimate child would often see the mother ostracised by not only the local community but by society at large. Baby farmers were therefore seen to be providing a useful service and were overlooked by the authorities.

The police were called in by the Salvation Army Major and PC Edgar Green promptly arrived accompanied by a Dr Buist. The baby was examined, found to be about six weeks old and well nourished. The following day though the baby's condition deteriorated and he began to suffer from vomiting and diarrhoea. The child was taken to the Union Workhouse where he was diagnosed as suffering from exposure. The child would hang onto life for a week but he died on 15 May 1907.

The day after she had abandoned the baby Rhoda had picked up another child. This time from Mr Stanley Rees whom she met at the train station at Pontypool. The man was good to his word and handed over £5 to Rhoda, with a promise to pay the remaining money in a week. Rhoda now though had a problem. She could not return to David Evans with a different baby and would have to find somewhere else to live. The answer came when she saw a notice in the window of a newsagents in Cardiff. And so it was that Rhoda took lodgings at 132 Portmanmoor Road. She told her new landlady, Hannah Wilson, that her name was Leslie James and that she had in her care the child of a friend who had recently fallen on bad times and could not care for the child. As well as lodgings for herself she was looking for someone to adopt the baby. Hannah Wilson said that she herself was childless and would be interested in taking in a child herself, and so that evening Rhoda gave the baby to the delighted Hannah Wilson, who handed over £1 for Rhoda's troubles.

This now left Rhoda free to take in other children for financial payments, and after arranging to have her mail forwarded to her new address she received another two letters. The first was from Stanley Rees who informed Rhoda that his job offer had fallen through, and that he would now require his baby back. The second letter was from

Lydia English who explained that the baby had now been born and was ready to be handed over to Rhoda, together with the cash sum agreed.

A day later Rhoda travelled to Fleur-de-lis and picked up the new-born child from Lydia English together with a cash payment of £5. One can only imagine how troubled Rhoda must have been as she travelled back to Cardiff, with yet another baby child in her care. Her landlady was delighted with the baby Rhoda had given her, but soon Rhoda would have to explain that that child's parents wanted the baby back. It was around 8 pm that night that Rhoda entered her lodgings, carrying a small parcel.

The following day Rhoda left the house early in the morning and when she returned she was so drunk that Hannah Wilson had to help her to bed. It was the following morning when Hannah went to check on Rhoda and found her still in bed, looking dreadfully hung over. When she tried to see to Rhoda she noticed the small package under the bed. Upon looking inside the package Hannah Wilson has the shock of her life to find it was a young baby and that it was dead.

'Hush don't say anything,' Rhoda told her landlady. 'I will get rid of it tonight.'

'Oh my God,' Hannah shouted and ran from the room. 'I will report you for this.' She went directly to the police and reported the incident to a Detective Inspector William Davey.

'I am not going to stand the blame for this,' Rhoda, still using the name Leslie James, told the policeman. 'Someone else is in this as well'

At the police station Rhoda was formally charged under the name of Leslie James with the murder of an infant child. 'I did not do it,' she replied.

On 6 June of that year, Rhoda appeared before magistrates and was remanded in custody on a charge of manslaughter. The following day the inquest on the child opened, and it was revealed that it had been smothered to death. And then a week later Rhoda's charge was upgraded to that of murder and she was informed that she would face trial sometime the following month.

By 23 July 1907, when the case finally came to court, there had been a major development. The baby that had been left with Hannah Wilson was now back with its rightful parents, after the police had visited Stanley Rees and told him of the child's whereabouts. The police investigation had been thorough, with all of the major players contacted, and yet when Rhoda stood in court and faced the judge and jury, it was under the name of Leslie James.

The defence said that the child had been ill and had died from natural causes, but the medical evidence against this suggestion was far too strong. The matter of the baby who had been left on the doorstep of Major Chatterton was also brought up, with the note that had been left with the baby produced in court. Although Rhoda had tried to hide the fact that she had written the letter, with the misspellings and bad grammar, she had not in fact disguised her own handwriting. Experts were able to compare samples of Rhoda's handwriting with the note and state with authority that they were one and the same. It seemed that Rhoda was not only responsible for the murder of one baby but also the death of another. The prosecution made the case that the first baby's death of exposure was a direct result of it being abandoned by this cold-hearted woman.

The evidence against Rhoda was compelling and it took the jury only twelve minutes to return the verdict of guilty of wilful murder. It was after the trial that it was finally revealed that the woman's name was actually Rhoda Willis, but by now she was sitting in a cell waiting for her execution. During the early hours of 14 August that year Rhoda asked to speak to her solicitor, where she confessed to her crimes, saying she could now meet her maker with a clear conscience. And then at 8 am that morning she was led to the scaffold and the sentence was carried out.

Child Murder in Pentre

On 29 April 1949, thirteen year-old Valerie Williams was murdered by her own mother. How could this be, the shocked community asked. Linda Williams had doted on her daughter. The woman had lost her husband, William, in 1944 and the young girl was the most important thing in her life. Why then did the devoted mother kill her own daughter? The answers make for a heartbreaking story.

Valerie had been a tall, attractive girl who attended Bronllwyn school in Gelli, and by all accounts she was a popular student, liked by both her classmates and teachers. On Friday 29 April 1949, the girl had come home from school proudly holding a letter she had written to send to relatives in Australia. She showed her mother the letter and they decided they would take it to the post office in the morning. Sadly this would not happen. By the following morning, Valerie would be dead.

Mrs Graff, the lodger had lived with the Williams family for the past three years, and when she woke on Saturday 30 April, she made herself a cup of tea and as was usual made one for Mrs Williams. She took it upstairs to the bedroom her landlady shared with her daughter. The bedroom door was locked and when Mrs Graff knocked, she was told to go away. This was strange behaviour from Linda Williams and Mrs Graff was sufficiently concerned to go around to Mrs Williams's sister's house which was only two streets away.

When the two women arrived back at Linda's house they found that Linda was now sat at the kitchen table, half dressed and visibly upset.

'Valerie is upstairs,' Linda told her sister. 'She is dead.'

The police were called and when they arrived they found the girl lying dead in her bed. There were no signs of violence but there was a strong smell of gas in the bedroom. There was a quilt nailed over the window and another over the mantelpiece and held down with bricks on the grate. When this was removed, police discovered that a pillow had been stuffed up the chimney. There was a gas bracket on the wall and to this a rubber tube had been attached. There were also sleeping pills scattered over the bedside cabinet. The eventual inquest would reveal that Valerie had died from carbon monoxide poisoning, and Mrs Linda Williams was charged with the murder of her daughter.

As the police led Mrs Williams away they were all of heavy hearts, for two suicide notes had been found. The notes painted such a desolate picture, that it was impossible not to feel sympathy for the woman who had killed her own daughter. The first note, addressed to Mrs Williams's sister, read:

I can not carry on any longer. I have tried to fight my nerves. I did not know what I was doing only I never told anyone for fear they would send me down there [meaning the much-feared Hensol Asylum]. Life is not worth living when like this everyday. I have ruined Valerie's nerves and I am afraid if I leave her she will end up down there. So I am taking her with me, because people would only point her out and her life would not be worth living. So we are going to Will [the late William Williams] and won't worry anyone. I know that God will forgive me sbecause he knows how hard I have tried to come better. I hope that God will never give you a nervous breakdown. Goodbye everybody. Bury us with Will. Now I know we are at rest. My insurance will bury us [sic].

Valerie Williams, pictured a month before her death. (*Evening News*)

The second letter was written to a friend, a Mrs Tegan of Avondale Road, Gelli and read: 'Forgive me for what I have done. I cannot carry on and I want to thank you for your kindness. Goodbye my dear and look after yourself. I can not leave Valerie. I love her too much.'

It would become clear that Mrs Williams had suffered a nervous breakdown sometime following the death of her husband almost five years previously, and had tried to live with the dreadful illness out of fear of being committed to Hensol Asylum, a mental institution housed in a gothic-style mansion in nearby Miskin. Billed as a colony for the mentally defective, the imposing building was a source of terror to many, and wild stories were told of what went on behind its walls. During this period there was a stigma attached to mental illness, and many believed that it was a source of shame to for anyone to suffer in such a way, almost as if it signified a weakness of character. Taking her own life seemed the only way out for Mrs Williams, though her plans went wrong and she herself survived the suicide attempt while her daughter had died in her sleep. Mrs Williams would inform the police that she had given her daughter sleeping pills before climbing into bed herself. Found guilty of the murder of her daughter, but judged to be insane, Linda Williams would indeed spend the rest of her days at Hensol Asylum.

Chapter 9

A Desire to Kill

If it can be said that true evil can exist, that it can be a motive for murder without any extenuating circumstances, then a charge of such nefariousness can be made against fifteen-year-old killer Harold Jones. This young man came from a solid working-class family and was popular with all who knew him, yet he would be compelled to kill for no other reason than the depraved pleasure afforded him by such monstrous actions.

The weather was good: it had been an exceptionally mild January and by 5 February 1921 there had been no real change. At this time of year the town of Abertillery would have

Harold Jones standing in the doorway of Mortimer's Corn Store. (*Courtesy Neil Milkins*)

been expecting to be facing bitter winds, bringing a bone-numbing chill and painting the town in translucent frost; not to mention the torrential rain, which often seems ubiquitous in the Welsh valleys. Instead men were going about in their shirtsleeves and children played in the streets without the burden of thick winter coats.

On that Saturday morning, Fred Burnell was in his kitchen at Earl Street, preparing food for his chickens. He had a saucepan on the stove, in which he was boiling up corn. He realized he was out of grit, an all-important ingredient in his poultry mix, and given the clement weather, and the corn store being only a street away, he decided to send his eight-year-old daughter Freda on an errand. He gave the girl a shilling, and an extra tuppence for herself and told her to go to Mortimer's store and purchase a bag of poultry grit and a little poultry spice.

'Be quick and you'll get an extra penny pocket money,' Mr Burnell told his daughter as she left the house, eager to run her errand. At that moment the father could not have known that this was the last time he would see his daughter's angelic face smiling back at him.

She would never be seen alive again.

Thirty minutes later and Mr Burnell wondered what had become of his daughter. The errand should have taken her all of ten minutes and yet she still hadn't returned and as the clock struck ten, Mr Burnell decided to go in search of his daughter. When he arrived at Mortimer's store, he glanced through the window but did not go inside to enquire if his daughter had been in. Instead he continued to the Co-operative Store, which also sold poultry food, and this time he went inside and asked if his daughter had been there. He was told that she hadn't been seen that morning.

By now Mr Burnell was starting to panic. He visited the town crier who then went around the town announcing, that Freda had disappeared and that anyone who saw her should inform her parents. At around one o'clock that afternoon, the police were informed of the little girl's disappearance and soon a search was organized, with the police joined by masses of volunteers from the town. As darkness fell, the search party equipped themselves with lamps from the local collieries, and it was reported that twinkling lights could be seen throughout the night as the hillsides were searched.

Sunday morning came with no sign of the girl and by now people were starting to fear that something terrible had happened. The previous night all of the cinemas in the area had flashed up a description of the clothing Freda Burnell had been wearing when she'd vanished.

> She was last seen wearing a red serge cap with blue velvet underneath, a brown coat, a blue turnover with white stripes, a brown jersey, new combinations, black stockings and black buttoned boots. Her hair was tied up in rags and she was carrying a small chocolate-coloured bag of American leather, 10-15 inches wide and rather deeper. She had a fresh complexion, blue eyes and light brown hair. She was somewhat small for her age and weighed about three and a half stone.

Only one person came forward as a result of the cinema announcements. Mary Ann Whiltshire said that she thought she had seen the girl going past her house at a little after nine o'clock the previous morning. Freda would have passed the woman's house on the way to the seed shop and the woman's evidence backed up the timing of when Mr Burnell said his daughter had left the house. When the police visited Mortimer's shop they were told by a live-in domestic servant named Doris Hathaway that Freda had indeed been into the shop that Saturday morning and that she had been served by the shop assistant, fifteen-year-old Harold Jones. When Harold was questioned by police he confirmed that he had served the girl with a bag of spice. She had also asked for some poultry grit but Harold told her that they didn't have any bags but they did have loose grit. The little girl then left the shop, saying she would ask her father if loose grit would suffice. The boy said he didn't notice which way the girl went after leaving the shop.

At a little after 7 am on that Sunday morning, collier Edward Thomas was on his way to work when he came across the body of the missing girl. Freda Burnell had been found in a lane to the rear of Duke Street, less than three hundred yards from her home. It would emerge that she had suffered a blow to the head and had been, what was termed rather euphemistically, outraged. The cause of death was established to be suffocation and the girl had been found with a scarf still tied around her throat.

The initial police investigation concentrated on an old barn which was situated close to where the body was found, and it was thought that she had been killed in the barn and then dumped in the lane at a later time. This would be proved to be not the case, which left the police baffled and on the Monday following Freda Burnell's death the Abertillery constabulary were joined by two detectives who had come down from Scotland Yard, Detective Chief Inspector Albert Helden, and Detective Sergeant Alfred Soden. These men were considered the cream of the country's detectives and were famed for capturing the culprit in a high-profile murder in Abergavenny which took place the previous year. Known as the Rose Cottage Mystery, the case saw Sarah Ann White murdered by her fifteen-year-old niece. Police had been baffled and it had taken diligent detective work by Helden and Soden to discover the killer had been the deceased's own niece.

The following Thursday, with the culprit still at large, the town saw the funeral of little Freda Burnell. As the procession moved through the streets, hordes of onlookers had gathered and they all bowed their heads in respect as the cortège went past. At the graveside service Brigadier Thomas Cloud of the Salvation Army addressed the mourners, saying: 'Satan has devoured the man who has done this thing and he has become a demonic worse than the Gadarene Demonic.' This is a reference from Luke, 8:26-39 which speaks of a man possessed by demons.

The town of Abertillery shut down: the roads were closed to

The funeral of Freda Burnell. (*Western Mail*)

all traffic other than the funeral procession and local businesses locked up for the day as a mark of respect. As the little girl's coffin was lowered into the ground Freda's friends from school lined up and one by one they threw flowers into the grave, tears running down their cheeks and falling onto the ground. The Union District Council had promised to pay for the funeral and eventually a grand headstone would be placed on the grave.

During the funeral someone from the village, a person who remains unknown, came up to Detective Chief Inspector Helden and told of the small storage shed which was owned by the storekeeper, Mortimer. The shed was situated only a few hundred yards from where Freda had been found. This would provide the police with a major breakthrough.

'Yes that was my daughter's,' Fred Burnell told the police as they showed him the handkerchief they had found in Mortimer's storage shed. 'There is chalk still upon it from where she used it to wipe the blackboard.'

The handkerchief had been found on the floor of the shed and the police were now convinced that this was where poor Freda had met her death. A wooden axe handle was also found and police believed this had been used to deliver the blow to the young girl's head, likely knocking her unconscious. This made sense of the fact that several neighbours had reported a brief scream on that Sunday morning. Had Freda, suddenly realizing that she was in danger, screamed for help and then been silenced with a blow to the skull from the heavy handle?

The investigation now turned to Harold Jones, with the two detectives becoming convinced that it was he who had killed the young girl. Harold had served her in the store, had been the last person to see her alive and had easy access to the storage shed. Now that the shed had been thoroughly searched it had been positively identified as being the scene of the crime. There was no question of that.

The inquest into Freda Burnell's death had opened on 8 February but was adjourned for her funeral. By the time the inquest resumed on

12 February, the two Scotland Yard detectives had returned to London, though they had given their evidence and theories about Harold Jones to the Abertillery police. It was this theory, the suspicion that Harold Jones had committed the crime, that was the focus of the inquest.

Many witnesses took the stand. Freda's father Fred looked weakened as he explained the circumstances that led up to the disappearance of his daughter. Several times he had to be helped as it looked as if his legs would buckle beneath him. His wife was equally distraught as she gave evidence which was mostly concerned with identifying the handkerchief which had been found in Mortimer's shed. Francis Gilbert Mortimer, the ten-year-old son of the store owner, then gave

Mortimer's storage shed. This photograph was taken by Detective Inspector William McBride. Note that the handkerchief circled is not the one Freda used, but was placed there for the purpose of the photograph to show the exact spot where the actual handkerchief had been discovered. (*Courtesy Neil Milkins*)

his own evidence. He told the court that on the morning that Freda had disappeared, he had accompanied Harold Jones to the storage shed in order to collect a sack of potatoes. Jones had told the young boy to remain outside while he went in and loaded the potatoes onto the trolley. This was around 10.15 am. The police theory was that the young girl's body had been in the shed at that time, and that Harold had made the young boy wait outside for obvious reasons.

'Was the shed door opened wide?' the Coroner asked the witness.

'Not very wide.'

'Was something preventing the door from being opened wide?'

'A sack.'

'Was it a full or empty sack?'

'Full.'

'Of what?'

'I do not know.'

'Have you ever gone with Harold to fetch potatoes before?' the coroner asked, changing the course of questioning slightly.

'Yes.'

'Have you always waited outside the shed while Harold went in?'

'No.'

'After the potatoes were put on the trolley what did Harold say?'

'You go on.'

'Do you ever remember him telling you to go on before?'

'No.'

A juryman then asked if it was normal practice for the trolley to be left outside the shed and the potatoes brought to it, rather than taking the trolley to the goods which would seem a more logical way to do things. To which the young boy responded that in the past the trolley had always been taken into the shed to be loaded up. Then one of the jury commented, 'Jones had never asked Francis Mortimer in the past to wait outside.'

The young boy's father Herbert Henry Mortimer, then took the stand. He seemed convinced that Harold Jones could not have carried out such a dreadful crime. He was vague with his answers, and was at pains to convince the jury that Harold Jones had been in the shop at the time it was said Freda Burnell had met her death. He admitted that he hadn't physically seen his errand boy but said he had heard Jones upstairs in the store 'moving around like a cart horse'.

The inquest went on until 7 March when the jury returned a verdict that the girl had been murdered by some person or persons unknown. During the inquest it had been made clear that only Herbert Mortimer, his family and his employers who had access to the storage shed. Everyone's movements had been thoroughly checked and it was certain that they could not have entered the shed, which left only Harold Jones. He had a window of opportunity between 9.15 and 9.40 on the morning of 5 February when no one had seen him in Mortimer's store.

Harold Jones had taken the stand several times during the inquest, being confident, at times overly so, but he had changed his story several times which prompted the coroner to scold him and remind him to tell the truth. He had explained his time away from the store by saying he had gone to purchase cigarettes at the local tobacconists. This had been proven to be true but it still, in the opinion of the police, gave Harold time to have abducted and killed the girl. He was detained following the closure of the inquest, and by that evening the two detectives from Scotland Yard had returned and were present when Harold Jones was formally arrested and charged with murder.

'I know it looks all black against me but I never done it.' Jones replied to the charge.

Harold Jones was remanded in custody until 5 April when he appeared before magistrates. It was decided that he should face trial on a charge of wilful murder and given the seriousness of the charges bail was refused. Jones was led away to Usk Prison. He would remain there until the next sitting of the Assizes at Monmouth.

The people of Abertillery could not, indeed would not, believe that one of their own could have done such a wicked deed, it was even more unbelievable that the killer could have been a fifteen-year-old boy. Harold Jones was well thought of in the community, his old schoolteachers had spoken of his good character and support groups had been formed in the town to protest his innocence. The police must have gotten it wrong. Surely, Harold Jones, a smart, well-spoken local boy, could not have done such a thing!

The trial of Harold Jones opened at Monmouth Assizes on 20 June 1921, a Monday. The town was filled to capacity for the hearing with people coming from all over hoping to catch a glimpse of the accused. The case had become infamous across the country and had been reported in newspapers as far away as America. This presented problems for the security of the prisoner, and Jones arrived at the hearing in a closed bus instead of the usual prison van.

The jury was sworn in and then the prosecution opened the proceedings with the case being made by Charles Francis Vachell KC. In a two-hour opening speech, he told of the events that took place on 5 February and of the subsequent investigation into the death of Freda Burnell. The court then broke for lunch and when proceedings resumed, Mr Lort-Williams KC cross examined many of the witnesses. This took up the rest of the first day and afterwards Harold Jones was returned to Usk Prison.

On the second day of the trial, just as proceedings where about to begin there was a yell of 'Hello son' from the rear of the court. Harold Jones looked up and with a smile, replied, 'Hello mam.' Mrs Jones then left the gallery, presumably unable to stand seeing her son in the dock. The prosecution then cross-examined Herbert Mortimer. At the earlier inquest, he had often stumbled over his words and been evasive but this time he held his own against the relentless cross-examination. He was still convinced of his errand boy's innocence and was at pains to demonstrate his belief to the court.

The third day of the hearing saw Harold Jones's father take to the stand to give his evidence. Phillip Jones told the court that his son's character in regard to sexual matters had always been good. He said it was impossible for Harold to have left the house on that Saturday night in order to move Freda's body from the storage shed and place it in the lane as the police believed. He would have known if Harold had gone out. Harold's mother then took the stand and corroborated her husband's evidence. She ended by saying that Harold had always been a good boy in regards to his behaviour towards young girls.

Walter Walters, the headmaster of the local school, told the court that Harold had been an exemplary pupil, and none of his teachers had ever had any concerns about his behaviour and general character. The rest of the day was spent hearing witness after witness extolling the virtues of Harold Jones. The jury must have been perplexed. The prosecution had been convincing in setting out their case against the young boy, but now he was being made to sound like a perfect young man by those who knew him best. He could not be guilty of this dreadful act. Harold Jones was an upstanding young man – he had been happy at school, playing cricket and football with some skill. He had the usual boyish companions, he smoked a little but did not drink at all. And he loved to read, adventure stories and detective tales being his favourites. He played the organ well, often did so at church and had ambitions of becoming a professional boxer.

On the fourth and final day of the trial there was a sizeable increase in the crowds outside the court. When Harold emerged from the prison bus he gave the gathered crowds a confident smile. Today his fate would be decided and he seemed nonplussed at the gravity of the situation he was facing.

'My Lord, we find the prisoner not guilty,' the foreman of the jury would tell the hushed courtroom. 'We find the prisoner not guilty and that is the verdict of us all.'

Harold Jones was immediately released from the dock and he made his way upstairs to the public gallery for a tearful reunion with his parents. Afterwards a large crowd were waiting outside as Jones emerged from the building. He was immediately swamped by friends and well wishers and they escorted him to chants of 'For he's a jolly good fellow' to a local restaurant. At the feast Harold Jones climbed onto a table and addressed his supporters with a speech: 'I thank you all. I do not hold a grudge against the people of Abertillery for the horrendous ordeal I have been put through.' Treated like some kind of war hero, Harold Jones was escorted back to Abertillery to find the streets filled with crowds of cheering well-wishers. Buntings and flags were hung from building to building and some reports state that Jones was presented with a gold watch by the head of the town council.

The people of Abertillery were certain that Harold Jones, this smart young man, could not have carried out the murder and yet two weeks after he had been found innocent, he was once again arrested, this time charged with the murder of eleven-year-old Florence Little. The girl's address had been 4 Darran Road, Harold lived at Number 10 and it was in Harold's house that her body had been found. Following the news of Harold's arrest, a crowd of more than 500 people gathered outside the police station, demanding that Jones be released. Things got so heated that Superintendent Henry Lewis had to address the crowd: 'I have found the body of the child in the attic of Harold Jones, foully murdered

Harold Jones pictured shortly after his acquittal of the murder of Freda Burnell. (*The Daily Sketch*)

and I have arrested Harold Jones. I think this is all I can tell you and it would help us if you disperse and go to your homes.'

The facts were that on the evening of Friday, 8 July 1921, Florence Little had been playing in the street outside her home in Darran Road. George Little, the girl's father, said he had seen her playing hopscotch shortly after supper with Flossie, the sister of Harold Jones. He had gone back into the house and then when he went back outside a short while later his daughter was nowhere to be seen. At around ten o'clock, Mrs Little went down the street to Number 10 and knocked on the door, thinking her daughter had gone to Flossie's home to play. Harold Jones answered the door, he was wiping his hands and said he had been bathing. He told the worried woman that her daughter had been there earlier but had left some time ago.

The following morning, after a frantic all-night search, the police decided to search Harold Jones's house, and in doing so found the body of the missing girl in the attic. Her throat had been slit and her clothing was saturated in blood. The investigation revealed that the girl had been killed in the kitchen, her throat slit and her head held over the sink until there was very little blood left in her body. Afterwards she had been manhandled up into the attic space, presumably to be disposed of when the opportunity presented itself. Eagle-eyed policemen noticed scuff marks around the attic trapdoor as well as a small amount of blood on the floor directly beneath, which led them to their grisly discovery.

When the police found the body of the girl she was partly dressed, a terrible gash on the right side of her throat which had undoubtedly

The body of Florence Little is removed from 10 Darran Road. (*Western Mail*)

Number 10 Darran Road as it is today. (*Author's collection*)

been done with a sharp instrument and there was a rope, of the kind used to tie packing crates, looped under the girl's arms. The initial examination of the body revealed bruises on the girl's temple but there was no sign that any sexual activity had occurred.

This time there was little doubt of Harold Jones's guilt and the town of Abertillery went into deep shock. Earlier they had been furious at the police for arresting Harold Jones and now many of them would have willingly killed the boy with their bare hands. Indeed there were angry scenes when a crowd appeared outside Jones's house, and the police had to intervene to stop several people entering. Jones had already been taken away, the crowd were told. The only people allowed to enter the house were the police and the investigation team, while the

Jones family had gone to stay with relatives nearby. Shortly afterwards Mortimer's store closed down and the Mortimers left town, plagued by the knowledge that it was largely the testimony of Herbert Mortimer that had saved Harold Jones from a guilty verdict during the earlier trial for the murder of Freda Burnell. If it was not for this testimony then there was a very good chance that Florence Little may have still been alive.

Incredible scenes at the funeral of Florence Little. (*Western Mail*)

On 13 July Florence Little's funeral took place and there were incredible scenes as more than 100,000 people came to the small Welsh town. The funeral cortège was two miles long, the flowers sent to the graveside formed a mound of colour amongst the grim proceedings and the entire town fell silent, united in grief.

The eyes of not only Wales but the world were on Abertillery. Shortly after the funeral of Florence Little an article was published in *The Sunday Chronicle*. Written by the English journalist Nettie Lewis under the pen-name of 'Jane Doe', the article was seen as criticism of those who had attended the poor girl's funeral.

The town that has been ravaged by some wild beast. The wild beast whose prey is little children. The wild beast who has laid a dread and icy claw around the hearts of all true mothers. They call it Abertillery.

But not a fresh of breath air fanned the perspiring colliery town last Wednesday; not a drop of cool, refreshing rain came to soothe the thirsty streets or the parched throats of the streams. Charabancs, trains, traps, buses, motorcars, disgorged their hot freights into the dirty streets … women in gay summer frocks, children in their best. Idle men with picnic baskets. Mother's carrying young babies and feeding bottles … some suckling as they surged along for a vantage point by the road side leading to Aberbeeg. Incredible crowds, incredible heat. An incredible numbers of babies and children. Nurses sponging the faces of women laying prone on the baked flagstones of side turnings. A cheerful holiday air or expectancy on faces … looking forward to something … something was going to happen that afternoon … something that would feed many a back-fence conversation to come. Only the bunting and flags were missing to make it the triumphal route of a smiling prince or a circus. But this was the funeral of Florence Little. The poor little girl who was hurried out of life by some wild beast.

The article went onto accuse the onlookers at the funeral of gawking, of putting their own children at risk amongst the surging crowds and of treating the solemn event as an entertainment. Once section stated: 'Abertillery. Your newspaper files have weekly records of crimes unspeakable – child assault, incest, and child vandalism appear to be commonplace events in your daily life.' The article seemed to suggest that it was not only Harold Jones on trial but the town of Abertillery itself.

The inquest into the death of Florence Little, having been adjourned for the funeral, resumed on 21 July. Superintendent Lewis told journalists that no photographs were to be taken in courtroom after a photograph of Harold Jones, taken at the opening of the inquest, had appeared in the *Sunday Chronicle*. Anyone seen brandishing a camera, the policeman warned, would be removed from the proceedings and quite likely be charged with contempt of court.

Harold Jones arrived from Usk and stood in the dock at 10.15, still maintaining his innocence. He stood there impassive as witness after witness was called to the stand. One young witness, eleven-year-old Ivy Pavey, told the court that she had been playing outside Powell's shop, which was situated at no 19 Darran Road, when she saw Flossie Jones go into the shop and emerge with a bottle of pop which she took back to her own house. After a few minutes Flossie came back out and told Florence Little that Harold wanted her in the house. The girl then said that she had seen both girls enter the house, and a few moments later Flossie came out alone and went to her Uncle Arthur's house. The girl said she did not see Florence again after she had entered the house at 10 Darran Road.

As more witnesses were called it became clear that all of the testimony placed Harold Jones alone in the house at the time that Florence Little was killed, and there was also strong physical evidence that connected Harold to the murder. The inquest would close on 22 July and Harold Jones was charged with wilful murder. He would be remanded in custody to face trial at the Monmouth Assizes. At this point Jones was still pleading his innocence.

On 27 October, less than a week before his trial was due to begin, Harold Jones confessed to the murder of both Florence Little and Freda Burnell. This was undoubtedly a tactic to avoid the death penalty. Harold was fast approaching his sixteenth birthday, and if the resulting trial continued after it and he was found guilty, then the only sentence available would be death. However, still being fifteen when he confessed, thus ensuring a swift trial, he would instead face life imprisonment.

On 1 November, the trial opened with Harold Jones immediately entering a plea of guilty to murder. The judge advised Jones not to plead yet, for his mental capacity had yet to be established. It could be manslaughter on the grounds of insanity, but at the point Mr Micklethwait, who was leading the defence team, spoke up:

My Lord, on behalf of my client I have to ask you to accept the plea. As you see from the calendar, the boy is fifteen years and nine months old, and as you are aware at this age, according to the 'Children's Act', accepting a plea of guilty means your Lordship may pass a sentence that he be detained at His Majesty's Pleasure. On the other hand, if the trial went over and beyond his sixteenth birthday then other circumstances could and might ensue.

There was much argument from both the prosecution and defence, but eventually the judge accepted the plea and sentenced Harold Jones to be detained at His Majesty's Pleasure. During this period a sentence such as this would mean that the prisoner could have his case reviewed every five years, but the judge was at pains to point out that the boy would serve at least ten years.

Once Harold Jones had been led from the dock, his confession, written whilst remanded in Usk Prison was read to the court. The statement, dated 17 September 1921, read:

I Harold Jones wilfully and deliberately murdered Freda Burnell in Mr Mortimer's warehouse on 5th February 1921. I also do confess that I wilfully and deliberately murdered Florence Little on 8th July, causing her to die without preparation to meet God. The reason for doing so being the desire to kill. Flora was about to leave the house when I got hold of her, seized her throat and cut her throat with a knife in the kitchen, putting over head over the sink. I then went to the front room, leaving Flora's body over the sink. I went back to the kitchen and wrapped a shirt around her head. I carried the body upstairs and placed it on a table beneath the entrance to the attic. I then got onto the table. I tried to lift the body into the attic but had to go outside and get a rope from the backyard. I then tied the rope around the body and got up into the attic myself and dragged the body up. After getting back onto the table, I replaced the cover to the attic and went downstairs to get a bowl of water and a cloth. I took it upstairs to wash the stains of blood off the walls, the landing and the table. I went downstairs to fetch a candle and finding more blood stains, I washed them off. I then went downstairs and threw the water from the bowl into the sink. Just as I was having a bath, Mrs Little came to the door. I denied that Flora was in the house and went back to my bath. I hereby declare the above statement to be true.

Harold Jones would be released from prison in 1941, and initially went to stay with an aunt in Berkshire. He would eventually marry and father a child, but he is known to have visited Abertillery several times – he was first sighted barely three months after his release when he visited a fish and chip shop in Somerset Street but he was recognized and quickly left, and then in 1946 he turned up again seeking an old relative but two men told him to get out of town, 'or else'. He did so but would return again and again. In the late 1940s, Jones attended a wedding at the Tabernacle Chapel and understandably was not made to feel welcome. Then in 1949, Hilda Snell was at the Brynithel Cemetary with her two granddaughters when she spotted Jones standing by the graves of the girls he had killed, both girls had been buried in close proximity. Jones is known to have visited his parents' new home at 14 Rhiw Parc Road and neighbours reported hearing him playing the organ. In June 1956 Jones was at the funeral of his father and again in 1960 Jones went into Abertillery's Glasgow Club but was recognized and quickly left. The final reported sighting of Jones in the town was in 1965 when he attended his mother's funeral.

Florence Little. (*Evening Express*)

Harold Jones lived until 1971 when he died of cancer. At that time he was living in London and going by the name of Harry Jones, but before died he told his wife that the name Harold Jones should be placed on his death certificate, a name he had not used for many years.

Possible Other Murders.

The Welsh author Neil Milkins has made a long investigation into Harold Jones and published two books on the subject, *Every Mother's Nightmare* (Old Bakehouse Publications, 2008) and *Who Was Jack the Stripper?: The Hammersmith Nudes Murders* (Rose Hayworth Press, 2011). The latter case concerned the killings of six women, possibly eight, between 1964 and 1965. The press dubbed the unknown killer 'Jack the Stripper' because each of his victims, all of them prostitutes, were left completely naked. Milkins makes a compelling, though largely circumstantial, case for Harold Jones having been the perpetrator of these crimes. The author manages to establish that Jones was living close to where the dead women were found, but other than that he fails to establish any tangible connection between Jones and the killings.

More likely are the 1946 rape and murder of eleven-year-old Muriel Drinkwater in Swansea, the rape and murder during the same year of eleven-year-old Sheila Martin in Kent and the 1959 murder of six year-old Cardiff schoolgirl Carol Stephens. Muriel Drinkwater was a farmer's daughter, who was raped and shot dead in woodlands close to her home. Sheila Martin was raped and strangled with her own hair-band in woodland near her home in Dartford, Kent. The third girl, Carol Stephens, went missing and was later found dead in woodland

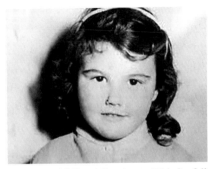

Six-year-old Carol Stephens. Did she fall victim to Harold Jones? (*Author's collection*)

in Llanelli. Witnesses said they saw Carol going off with a dark-haired man wearing a trilby, and driving a green car. None of the three cases has ever been solved but Jones was known to have visited his home town during the periods of the two Welsh murders, and his wanderings could have very well taken him to Kent. Did he once again feel the desire to kill and acted on this terrible urge by abducting these girls?

At the time of writing the police have closed the files to the public on all three cases, after a DNA breakthrough in which police managed to lift a familial DNA profile from a semen stain on a raincoat that Muriel Drinkwater had been wearing when she had been abducted. This gives a firm suggestion that all three cases are linked, and will hopefully see developments in the fullness of time. Could it be possible that Harold Jones had gone on killing after being released from prison?

Chapter 10

Depravity Beyond Imagination

The 1947 rape and murder of 76-year-old Rachel Allen in the Rhondda Valley caused such a sensation that Chief Detective Inspector John Capstick, the famed detective who headed up Scotland Yard's secretive Ghost Squad, was called in to bring the case to a swift conclusion. Capstick, accompanied by Detective Sergeant John Stoneman, arrived in the valleys on 12 October 1947, the day following the gruesome crime, and immediately went to work to bring the unknown perpetrator to book.

Capstick, known as 'Charlie Artful' by London's criminal underworld, had a reputation for always getting his man. He was a tenacious detective, who ran a string of informants which was why, following the Second World War, he was selected to head up the four-man team known as the Special Duties Squad or the 'Ghost Squad', in order to tackle the rampant post-war racketeering. 'Go out into the underworld. Gather your informants. Do whatever is necessary to ensure that the gangs are smashed up. We will never ask you to divulge your sources of information. But remember – you must succeed', were the orders given to this elite team of detectives.

Wattstown in 1947 was dominated by the coal industry. Residents faced a life of hardship, the men would spend their working time down the mines while the women had to struggle to bring up children on the meagre wages the mine owners paid the workforce. The weekends would see a brief respite from the working week and men and women would pack out the public houses and clubs.

Such was the scene on Saturday 11 October 1947 and the Butcher's Arms was doing a roaring trade when Rachel Allen, known locally as the washerwomen because she earned her living by taking in washing, walked into the Butcher's Arms Hotel. Rachel was a familiar figure at the hotel and she would sit alone, on a small bench in the passage, to consume several half-pint glasses of strong Welsh beer. An eccentric character, she was well known and patrons of the hotel would often buy her a drink and bring it out to her in the passageway. During that evening, Rachel went to the bar to get herself another drink when she whispered something in the ear of Evan Evans who was drinking with another man, Tom Phillips. Whatever it was she had said, it appeared to anger Evans and he told the woman to 'Bugger off'.

Afterward Evans and Phillips left the hotel together but when Phillips stopped to talk to a man, Evans wandered off alone. This was around 10 pm and a quarter of a hour later a woman, identified as Mrs Harper, was walking up Heol Llechau, the street on which the Butcher's Arms was situated, when she heard Rachel Allen shouting at someone outside her house, in Hillside Terrace which was only a street away. When she turned into the street, Mrs Harper saw a man dressed in a dark suit being chased down the street by the old washerwoman.

'If you don't go away from here, I'll report you to the police,' Rachel shouted after the retreating man. As far as it can be established Mrs Harper was the last person, other than the killer, to see Rachel Allen alive. For around a hour later Mrs Gertrude Morris was returning to her own home at 76a Hillside Terrace, when she stumbled over something on the ground. When she looked down she was horrified to discover the body of her next-door neighbour, Rachel Allen. The woman screamed, which brought several people from nearby houses to the gruesome scene.

The police soon arrived on the scene and finding the body horribly brutalised they secured the scene, and many uniformed officers and plainclothes detectives came into the village. During the period crimes of this nature were routinely reported to Scotland Yard, and the Welsh police were immediately ordered to keep the scene secure and await the arrival of a chief inspector who would take over the investigation.

The body was still *in situ* the following day when Chief Inspector John Capstick examined the scene. The remains lay in a pool of congealed blood, the woman's face had been battered and the injuries were such that her features were unrecognizable. Her clothing was in disarray with her skirt pulled up to her waist and her undergarments torn. A key, later established to be her front-door key, was clutched in her rigor-struck right hand, and there was a new tin of snuff on the ground besides her. The rest of the crime scene was carefully examined, blood samples were scraped off the front door of Rachel's home and sent to the forensic laboratory in Cardiff for detailed analysis, and only then were the remains of Rachel Allen transported from the scene to the mortuary at East Glamorgan Hospital in nearby Church Village.

The later post-mortem would reveal many injuries to the old woman's body. Her skull was fractured, her jaw and several ribs were broken and there were superficial injuries all over her face. Bizarrely a matchstick had been shoved into the woman's left nostril and it was clear she had been raped. Shock was believed to be the cause of death and the doctor was not sure if the rape had been committed while the woman was still alive, or if indeed she had been dead when the violation had taken place.

The community of Wattstown was subjected to questioning by the police, and an extended search was launched to locate a possible murder weapon. The snuffbox found besides the body had initially been believed to have been dropped by the killer, but Capstick soon discounted this, when he learned that Rachel Allen herself had bought the snuff from a general store immediately after leaving the Butcher's Arms that evening. The storekeeper, a Mrs Day, had served Rachel with the snuff and also, she told the detective, one sweet from the old woman's rations.

On the Tuesday following the murder Capstick, together with two other police officers, visited the home of 21-year-old Evan Evans at 39 Heol Lechau. Capstick had heard about the altercation between Rachel Allen and Evan Evans at the Butcher's Arms, and when the detective asked Evans about his movements between 10.15 and 11.20 on the night of Rachel's killing, he replied that he did not kill the woman and that he knew nothing about the murder. He stated that after leaving the Butcher's Arms he had gone straight home. However there was something about the man's manner that interested Capstick, and he asked Evans to accompany him to the police station for further questioning.

Once at the police station Capstick again asked Evans about his movements on the night in question and once again the man insisted that he had gone straight home from the Butcher's Arms. When asked what clothes he had been wearing that night, Evans replied that he was wearing the same blue suit that he now had on. He stated that this suit was the only one he owned. When asked about his shoes, he claimed not to remember which pair of shoes he had been wearing. He was currently wearing brown brogues but had a black pair at home. The detective had already been told that Evans had been wearing a brown suit on the night of the murder, and whilst Evans was being questioned Capstick sent another officer back to the man's home to collect his black shoes and whatever clothing that could be found.

'Your clothing will be microscopically tested for traces of blood,' Capstick told Evans who by this point was visibly nervous. The policeman noticed that Evans was clenching and unclenching his fists as if suffering great agitation. This told the detective that he had got his man, and now it was just a matter of proving it.

'I drank eight to ten pints at the Butcher's,' Evans told Capstick. 'It is difficult to recall events.'

Capstick nodded knowingly, and only had to sit back and wait. It was not long before Evans changed his story, admitting he was responsible for the death of the old lady. He claimed that he had accidentally bumped into Rachel on his way home from the Butcher's Arms. The old woman had fallen against a wall, the man said, and started cursing him, calling him a 'filthy pig'. Evans said he had then lost his temper and hit Rachel and she fell down onto the yard outside her house. The man went on to say that he had been in the grip of a fevered temper and had continued to hit the old woman while she was on the ground. He freely admitted he had kicked her several times in the face. He concluded by saying that he had then raped the old woman and after that he had gone home to the house he shared with his mother. He explained the blood over his suit to his mother by saying that he had been fighting. He told Capstick that the suit had been new that day and he also informed the policeman that the brown suit was currently hidden inside the sofa back at his house. Evans was then charged with murder and escorted to a cell at Ferndale police station. Then Capstick went back to Heol Llechau and sure enough he found the heavily bloodstained brown suit exactly where Evans had said it would be.

Evans faced trial at Cardiff on 15 December 1947, having been remanded in Cardiff Gaol since October, and the prosecution, led by J.F. Claxton, presented their case. They pointed out that Rachel Allen was a reclusive widow, whose husband had not returned from the Great War. She was said to live very frugally, existing on just £1 a week. There was little furniture in the home that she shared with several cats, no seemed sure just how many of the animals she had since she was always taking strays in, but it was believed to have been at least a dozen.

Chief Inspector Capstick, surrounded by police officers, leads Evan Evans into Porth Magistrates' Court. (*South Wales Echo*)

When the defence took to the stand all they offered was that Evans had been severely provoked. They said that Evans was suffering from psychological disturbances, caused by the death of his sister six months prior to the murder of Rachel Allen. It was said that Evans, a collier at the Lewis Merthyr pit in Porth, was a quiet, unassuming man and was of previous good character.

The judge in his summing up called the killing 'a filthy and callous murder'. And it took the jury just ten minutes to return a verdict of wilful murder. An appeal was announced and this was heard in January 1948, with the hopes of the defence being that the charge would be reduced to manslaughter which did not attract the death penalty. They were at great pains to point out that when Evans had stood in the witness box at his trial, he seemed unaware of the seriousness of his position, which suggested insanity. The appeal failed, however and the original verdict was upheld. And then on 3 February 1948, on a rain-soaked morning, Evans was led to the scaffold at Cardiff gaol and justice was served.

Chapter 11

Hired by a Killer

Picking up a violent fare is every taxi driver's worst fear, and for 58-year-old John Armstrong that fear was realized when on Friday, 5 October 1979, he picked up a passenger from the Fairwater Hotel in west Cardiff. The call had been made to the offices of Castle Cabs situated on Cardiff's Westgate Street, with a man giving his name as Williams and requesting a car be sent to pick him up and take him to Cowbridge. John Armstrong, better known as Jack, was driving the next available car and he was promptly sent to pick up Mr Williams.

At 1.35 pm, Jack radioed into his control, stating that he had picked up his passenger. This was the last anyone would hear of him and after a hour had gone by, Arnold Dickson, the manager of Castle Cabs, tried to reach Jack on the two-way radio but received no reply. The ride to Cowbridge should have taken no more than forty minutes there and back but Dickson assumed that Jack had taken a break for lunch. After another hour had passed Dickson did become concerned and he telephoned Jack's home, speaking to his wife Evelyn who told the cab operator that she had not heard from her husband since he had left for work earlier that day. Still no official alarm was raised because although Jack's disappearance was unusual, it was not unheard-of for a driver to suddenly go off the grid. Drivers had been known to pick people up without calling the fare in to control, keeping the money themselves in order to supplement their meagre wages. Although the taxi company was a private hire firm as opposed to a hackney business, which meant that technically picking up a passenger who hailed the cab from the side of the road was illegal, it did go on. It was part of the taxi business and drivers would often boast amongst themselves of the extra fares they had picked up – 'hobbling', they called it.

However at 4.45 that afternoon, Jack's cab, a 1975 metallic bronze Colt Sigma, was found abandoned at Treoes Lane, a secluded spot next to the Waterton Industrial Estate on the outskirts of Bridgend. When the car had been found the doors were wide open and there was a lot of blood on the interior upholstery, which suggested that the cab had been the scene of a violent assault. Neither Jack Armstrong nor his mysterious passenger Williams were anywhere to be seen.

Fearing for the safety of Mr Armstrong, the South Wales Police immediately set up an incident room and a search party was organized. All in all the search party consisted of more than 400 police officers, as well as members of the army and the public. The police had decided that Jack Armstrong had not been in the cab when it reached Treoes Lane, the theory was that the passenger had thrown the driver out of the cab elsewhere and driven the vehicle himself. This meant that a large area of woodland between Bridgend and Cardiff had to be searched.

The search went on through the weekend, and when police discovered Mr Armstrong's driving license together with other documents wrapped in a bloody rag and thrown into a hedge close to where the vehicle had been abandoned, concerns for his safety were raised. The police now decided to treat the disappearance as a murder investigation and a second incident room was set up in Cardiff to handle evidence relating to the initial stage of the cab's fateful journey. Chief Superintendent Viv Brook now found himself heading up a case the like of which he had never dealt with in his long and distinguished career; the paperwork generated would be incredible and in all, during the course of the investigation, the police would interview more than 12,000 people, and follow numerous leads.

Mr Armstrong's body would be found on Monday 8 October, more than eleven miles away from where his taxi had been abandoned, partially covered by dense undergrowth at a lonely spot on Cowbridge Common. The taxi driver had been subjected to a frenzied attack. The leading pathologist (and now best-selling author of historical crime thrillers) Bernard Knight carried out the autopsy and would attribute the cause of death to extensive skull fractures which led to considerable damage to the brain. The weapon used is believed to have been a hammer, which fitted in with a description police had received describing Williams as a man dressed for work and carrying a tool-bag.

The police would wonder what the motive had been for the killing. The amount of money Mr Armstrong would have had on him had been estimated to have been between £10 and £20, hardly a fortune and certainly not even in 1979 to have been an amount worth killing for, surely. The most likely explanation seemed that there had been no motive, that an argument had somehow broken out within the taxi and ended with terrible consequences. Though given the extent of the injuries Mr Armstrong had received it was obvious that the entire beating had not taken place inside the vehicle. The theory then was that the passenger, known only as Williams, had tried to flee the vehicle without paying his fare but had been caught by Mr Armstrong who likely leapt from the taxi after the man. There had been a struggle and the passenger had pulled a hammer from his tool-bag and violently swung it against Armstrong's head, hitting him with three separate blows. The result would have been that the taxi driver would have been knocked senseless and death would have been mercifully quick. The man's skull had been caved in by the blows, the brain pierced by bone fragments. It was a shocking crime and highlighted the vulnerable position taxi drivers put themselves in each time they took to the road.

'Drivers are being very careful about the fares they pick up,' Stan Crouch, of Castle Cabs told the *South Wales Echo* following the discovery of Mr Armstrong's body. 'They tend to get nervous about out-of-town jobs and will remain so until this man is caught. Single male passengers are being asked to sit in the front of cabs. I know of two drivers who have gone to the expense of having reinforced Perspex screens installed between them and back seat passengers.'

There were suggestions in the press that taxi drivers should carry truncheons similar to those used by the police, particularly as the police had now changed their theory and believed the first blow was struck while the two men had been in the car. At a press conference held on the Wednesday following the discovery of Mr Armstrong's body the police held a press conference and told reporters that they believed Mr Armstrong had first been struck from behind after pulling over to the side of the road at Cowbridge Common. Then the killer dragged him from the car and finished him off with two further blows to the head, before driving off in the taxi cab. The motive, the police now believed, was robbery. Had the man called Williams ordered the taxi with the intention of killing and robbing the driver? If so this made him a particularly dangerous man and the police were desperate to bring the manhunt to a conclusion. Appeals were put out for witnesses who may have seen the man getting into the taxi at Fairwater or at any other time during the journey.

Many witnesses did come forward and the police were able to produce a photofit of the man called Williams, and this was released

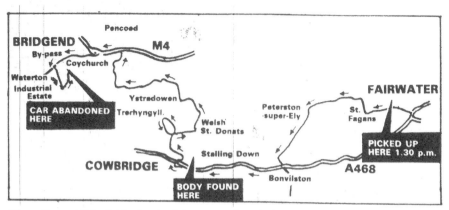

The police published this sketch of the route taken during the tragic journey that cost Jack Armstrong his life. (*South Wales Police*)

to the press together with a description stating that the man believed to be Williams was around thirty years old with a slim build and collar length brown hair.

The police now believed that the man called Williams had thrown a tool-bag onto the back seats of the taxi at the Fairwater Hotel, and then climbed into the back himself. The car then drove off towards St Fagins and then went through St Brides and Peterson-Super-Ely, before joining the A48 at Sycamore Cross. From there the car did a right and drove towards Cowbridge Common. It was here that the attack took place with Mr Armstrong struck once while in the car, and then twice more whilst outside. His body was then thrown into a shallow ditch and covered with undergrowth. Next, the police believed, the killer had turned around on himself and driven the taxi cab down into Aberthin and along the Talbot Green Road, before taking the forestry road through Ystradowen before turning towards Welsh St. Donats and taking Watery Lane which took the car through Llansannor, City, St. Mary Hill and into Treoes Lane where the vehicle was abandoned. It was then believed that the killer made his escape by walking along an obscure lane into Coychurch. This all suggested that the man called Williams had a good knowledge of the area.

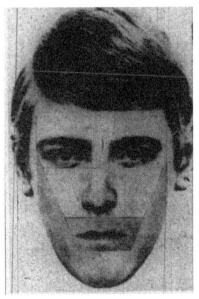

The biggest problem for the police was not a lack of leads but an abundance of leads and sightings to be checked up. One such lead even took detectives to France after police decided to talk to two girls who had been camping in the area close to

Police photofit of the man believed to have been Williams. (*South Wales Police*)

where Mr Armstrong's body had been found. It was believed that the man Williams had twice taken taxis to visit the girls at their campsite on Cowbridge Common. This had been in the weeks immediately prior to the murder of Jack Armstrong, and when the girls were eventually traced to Brittany the lead would, like many others in this tragic case, prove to yet another red herring.

Following several witness statements from people who swore they had seen the man in the photofit on the day of the murder, the police were soon to concentrate on the town of Brynna, but although there was high expectations of an imminent arrest, all leads ended up running into a brick wall. It was as if the killer, this man who had given the taxi firm the name of Williams, had simply vanished into thin air.

Twelve months later, on the anniversary of the killing, police staged a reconstruction of the fatal journey. The reason for this seemed not to be that the police had hopes of jogging someone's memory but more to reassure the public that they had not forgotten about Mr Armstrong. Eventually the investigation would wind down but the case still remains officially open in the files of the South Wales Police.

'Somebody must have seen him; he can't have just disappeared into thin air.' Chief Superintendent Brooke had told reporters only weeks after the murder, and yet that is precisely what seemed to have happened. Somehow the killer had simply walked away from the abandoned vehicle and vanished into, as the police officer put it, thin air.

Chapter 12

The Wrong Man

Jonathan Jones must have been incredibly nervous during the early months of 1996. The date of the appeal against his conviction for the execution-style killings of Harry and Megan Tooze, the elderly parents of his girlfriend Cheryl, grew ever closer. He had already served more than two years in prison, and if the appeal didn't go his way then it seemed likely that he had an intolerable future ahead of him. His faith in the justice system must have been shaken to the core, since he had been convicted on the flimsiest of evidence; indeed at the time of the murders of which he was accused he had been many miles away in London. That hadn't stopped the police building a case against him and ultimately convincing a jury of his guilt. At Jones's original trial the jury had, by a majority of ten to two, found him guilty of two counts of murder.

Jones had been sentenced to life imprisonment, and yet there had always been reasonable doubt over his guilt. This is reflected in the fact that following his conviction, the presiding judge, the late Sir Richard Rougier, had written to the then Home Secretary Michael Howard and expressed his concerns over the conviction. 'I am bound to record that the verdict caused me some surprise. There were undoubtedly many suspicious features about Jones's case, but at the same time many items of evidence upon which the prosecution relied as pointers to guilt had fallen decidedly flat.'

While researching this particular story for this book, I was told by a retired police detective, who wishes to remains nameless, that he himself had been shocked when the jury returned a guilty verdict.

In the former detective's own words, 'We never really had anything. Our case was so weak.' And the deeper I went into the facts, the more certain I became that Jonathan Jones should never have been a suspect in the first place. Did the fact that the police concentrated on Jones mean that other avenues of investigation were neglected? Is the real killer still out there, living an ordinary life while so many other lives have been wrecked by an act of incredible violence perpetrated one afternoon in 1993?

The known facts in the case are that on the morning of 26 July 1993 Harry and Megan Tooze had been in the Tesco's store at Talbot Green, and before returning home to the isolated Ty-ar-y-waun farmhouse on Llanharry meadow they had visited the local post office. This was around noon and at 1.30 pm a neighbour, Mrs Milsom-Gabe heard two gunshots but assumed it was Harry Tooze out shooting rabbits which was a regular occurrence. 'I knew he [Harry] had been having problems with rabbits eating his cabbages,' she told a reporter from the *South Wales Echo*. 'He had planted the whole garden with cabbages and the rabbits had taken them all so I knew he would shoot any rabbits he saw.' Those shots, though, were not the sound of an irate farmer shooting rabbits, but almost certainly the shots that had killed Harry Tooze and his wife, Megan. Both had been shot in the head at point-blank range and afterwards their bodies had been concealed in their cowshed while the killer or killers vanished into the surrounding countryside. Llanharry Meadow is a secluded area and there are several routes a killer could have taken without much chance of being observed.

It wasn't until that evening when the couple's daughter, Cheryl, who lived in Orpington in Kent tried to contact her parents by telephone that the alarm was raised. Cheryl grew concerned when her calls weren't answered, since she knew they should be at home watching *Coronation Street*; the soap opera was their favourite and they never missed an episode, so they should have been at home. Cheryl also knew that her father wasn't well, having recently suffered from a hernia and after telephoning the family doctor and the local hospital she decided to call a neighbour to ask if they would visit the farmhouse. Shortly afterwards she received a telephone call from Owen Hopkins, a farmer who lived nearby. Mr Hopkins told her that her parents were not at home, that their door was not locked and that there was food half-cooked in the oven. Cheryl then persuaded her fiancé, Jonathan Jones, to drive from Kent to the farmhouse in order to assist in finding the elderly couple. Cheryl remained at their home in Kent, as she had to be at work early in the morning and the couple reasoned that there would be a simple explanation for all this. The thought that her parents had been murdered would not have crossed her mind. Things like that just didn't happen in the quiet backwater that was Llanharry.

The police visited the farmhouse after being called by worried neighbours, but unaware that this was soon to turn into a murder investigation they failed to secure the property which meant that many feet, and not only those of the police force had trampled over potential evidence. It was later discovered that there had been a small pool of blood by the wooden gate that led into the farmyard but by the time this was discovered it was forensically useless.

Jonathan Jones meanwhile had left his home in Kent at around ten that night and would eventually arrive at the farmhouse at three in the morning. The duration of his drive would later raise concerns with the police as it shouldn't have taken five hours to make the 200-mile journey, but this was later explained by having visited two service stations, once to refuel and then later to telephone Cheryl. There was also the fact that the weather had been foul with heavy rain and Jonathan had been forced to drive at around 50 mph. All but the final six miles of the journey was motorway, and the South Wales stretch of the M4 can be notoriously difficult to negotiate in bad weather.

When Jonathan arrived at the farmhouse he was informed by police that the body of a male had been found in the cowshed. It was when the

Harry and Megan Tooze were both gunned down at point-blank range. (*Author's collection*)

police imparted this information to him that they became suspicious. Several officers felt that Jonathan Jones's reaction to the news was rather odd: he asked very few questions and didn't even ask if the body was that of his fiancée's father. Jonathan, though, would have been tired after his long drive and the bad news must have no doubt come as a complete shock. At the time he would have been stunned, and yet police took his reactions as a pointer to his guilt. The rain had been hammering down on the scene and Jones was led into the farmhouse by a police officer, where he was left alone in the sitting room for some time. It was in this sitting room that a cup was found that bore his fingerprints, or to be precise a partial thumbprint and it was this print that would provide the backbone to his eventual prosecution.

Jonathan Jones would learn the precise details as the night went on – now it was revealed that two bodies had been found in the cowshed, that of Mr Tooze and his wife. Harry had shot in the face and placed in a trough and covered with hay bales. Megan Tooze had been shot in the back of the head from a distance of about three feet: no doubt she had witnessed the death of her husband and had been trying to escape. Her body had then been placed in the cowshed and covered with a large roll of carpet. Whoever had committed the double murder had hidden the bodies well, which was why it had taken the police, who had been at the farmhouse since early evening, so long to find them. The first body found had been that of Harry Tooze and the police felt that suicide would turn out to be the explanation for what had happened which was why, they later claimed, the crime scene hadn't been immediately sealed off. Though when the second body was discovered the police realized that they were dealing with not just a murder, but a double murder.

Police forensic experts at the Tooze farmhouse. (*South Wales Echo*)

Shortly after arriving at the farmhouse, Jonathan telephoned Cheryl at home and gave her the terrible news about her parents, and she immediately made preparations to return to Wales herself. A chain of events now kicked in that Jones could not have foreseen and although police followed many lines of enquiry, pulling in several local men for questioning, they would ultimately turn their attention to Jonathan Jones. And in December, five months after the murders, the police charged him with the murder of Harry and Megan Tooze.

The police theory was that Jonathan Jones, without Cheryl's knowledge, had travelled down from Kent on the morning of 26 July, committed the murders in the afternoon and then travelled back to Kent, arriving at just after seven that evening. He had told Cheryl that he had been out all day looking for office premises for a market research firm that they were hoping to set up, but when the police tested his alibi they found several points of concern. Nevertheless, the only real evidence the police had to back their theory was the partial thumbprint of the accused that had been found on a china cup which was in the sitting room at the time of the murders. The motive was, the police felt, financial as Cheryl Tooze was the sole beneficiary of her parent's estate and was likely to inherit upwards of £150,000 upon the death of her parents.

'Don't be ridiculous,' Cheryl told police when they entered her home in Kent and ushered Jonathan through to the kitchen. The police had informed Cheryl that they were arresting her fiancé for the murder of her parents. Cheryl assumed that this was all a dreadful mistake, but several hours later the police again contacted her and told her Jonathan had now been formally charged and would remain in police custody. If the police felt that Cheryl Tooze would now see her fiancé for the cold-blooded killer they believed him to be, then they were sorely mistaken.

Not for one moment did Cheryl suspect him. She knew deep down in her heart that Jonathan was innocent, that the police were wrong and that the real killer or killers of her parents were still out there. She would stand by Jonathan every step of the way. She stood by Jonathan when he was charged, when he appeared at the magistrates' court, and when he finally sat trial at the Newport Crown Court. And even when the jury delivered a guilty verdict, Cheryl remained steadfast in her support. She immediately moved in with Jonathan's parents in nearby Caerphilly and set about a campaign to protest her fiancée's innocence.

'At first I wanted to die but I knew I must be strong for Jonathan,' Cheryl told the *Independent* newspaper following the conviction. 'Jonathan is the kindest person I have ever known. There is no way on God's earth that he would kill anybody, let alone two people that he loved. The people who killed my parents are out there and that is not right.'

Only days after the guilty verdict Cheryl put up a £25,000 reward for information leading to the arrest of the killer or killers of her parents. By doing so, she was making it known that she did not accept the verdict that her fiancée was guilty of the dreadful crimes, and that she would not rest until true justice was delivered.

That justice was partially realized at London's Royal Courts of Justice, when the appeal hearing was held on 10 May 1996. Jonathan Jones's conviction was quashed and the appeal court decided there was no evidence for him to sit a retrial. He was set free, but it would be a bittersweet victory for Jonathan and Cheryl both knew that the real killers were still out there.

The Court of Appeal had highlighted several issues of concern during the hearing, which had led to their decision to rule the conviction unsafe.

Cheryl Tooze and Jonathan Jones. Love would help them through their nightmare. (*Author's collection*)

Jonathan Jones's alibi was that he had been in Kent looking for office premises when the murders took place, and although this couldn't be proven during his original trial the defence had now found new evidence, in the shape of a till receipt, that proved beyond doubt that Jones had in fact been in Kent as he had stated. There was also the fact that the Crown had attempted to prove a financial motive for the killings but had in fact been unable to establish one, and it was claimed that the judge had misdirected the jury at the original trial. The thumbprint on the cup was also deemed to be useless as evidence since the print could have been placed on the cup at numerous times before the murder: it was also possible that Jones had touched it when he was alone in the farmhouse following the double murder. All in all there were twenty grounds for appeal and each of these was considered carefully before the court set Jonathan Jones free, exonerating him of the crimes of which he had been accused. Up to the present day the case remains unsolved, and despite several inquiries over the years and the discovery of the shotgun barrels used in the killings it looks as if the mystery will continue for the foreseeable future.

The Bullseye Killings

In May 2011, Pembrokeshire man John Cooper, known as the 'Bullseye Killer' due to the fact that he had once appeared on the television darts show of that name, was given four life sentences for a series of brutal shotgun murders carried out during the 1980s. Police were intrigued by similarities between Cooper's crimes and the Tooze murders and an investigation was launched to find any connection between Cooper and the killings at the Llanharry farmhouse. It seemed a promising direction given that Cooper was known from time to time to work as a farm labourer which could have brought him into contact with Harry Tooze, there was also the fact that Cooper had painted the barrel of a shotgun white. In 2011 two shotgun barrels, believed to have been those used in the Tooze murders were discovered in a flooded quarry close to the Tooze farmhouse. These too had been painted white.

South Wales Police have yet to make the findings of their inquiry into a possible connection between Cooper and the Tooze killings public. In fact despite several freedom of information requests, one made by myself while this book was being written, the police are refusing to release details of the findings of any

John Cooper as he appeared on *Bullseye*. (*ATV*)

of the multiple inquiries into the Tooze killings. They claim that doing so could jeopardise a future conviction for the murders of Harry and Megan Tooze.

Cooper is currently serving four life sentences for two double murders and the rape of a sixteen-year-old girl. He has an history of crime which included more than thirty robberies. This again makes him of interest in the Tooze case since a month before the Toozes were murdered, they suffered a burglary at their farmhouse in which a shotgun was stolen. Cooper was known to sell gold that he had stolen and the author of this book was told by a reliable source, who wished to remain nameless, that there was gossip around the village that suggested Harry Tooze was known to have fenced stolen gold. The information about the gold was not known by the police during the original investigation but the author of this book had now passed on the details to the police.

When Cooper was arrested the police discovered that he had kept a bucket filled with various kinds of keys which he had stolen during his many robberies. It is believed that this bucket is now in the possession of the Pembrokeshire police. Could any of these keys prove a connection to the Tooze farmhouse?

There is also the fact that John Cooper had strong links to the farming community, and had at times worked as a farm labourer. Could this have brought him into contact with Harry Tooze? There were sightings of Harry Tooze with a grey-haired man several weeks before the shootings, and the police were unable to locate this man, whose description matched John Cooper at this period.

Of course it is all speculation but it is a fact that some weeks before he was killed, Mr Tooze was heard having a furious argument with a man outside his farmhouse, but the police were unable to establish who this man had been. It is also fact that Mr Tooze kept a loaded Luger pistol in his house. The mere possession of a weapon such as this would earn gaol time, so Mr Tooze must have had a good reason for taking such a risk. Was he afraid of someone? Someone like John Cooper?

Chapter 13

Like Something out of a Horror Film

I t was just routine when on Friday 24 April 2015, Police Sergeant
Stuart Williams and PC Craig Gardner called on the home of
47-year-old Christopher May at Andrew's Court in Pontypridd.
They were making inquiries into the disappearance of a local woman,
Tracey Woodford, who had failed to return home after visiting the
town's Skinny Dog public house on the night of Tuesday, 21 April. The
police had spent the previous days establishing Tracey's movements
leading up to her disappearance and had realized that Christopher
May was the last person to have been seen with Tracey.

May and Tracey had left the public house together at 11.20 that
Tuesday night and were caught on CCTV camera as they walked along
the quiet streets of Pontypridd. They seemed happy enough, like any
other couple on their way home after visiting a pub. Indeed Tracey was
wearing May's coat. He had given it to her in a gentlemanly act to ward
off the night's chill.

And now on that Friday morning that same man stood in his doorway
and told police that he hadn't seen Tracey since Tuesday night, that she
had made her way home sometime after they had left the pub together.

'There was a stench of rotten meat coming from the flat,' Sergeant
Williams would later tell the court. 'And May seemed agitated, ill at
ease.' The policemen were suspicious and when they asked if they
could come in, May simply stood aside and allowed them to enter.

'It was like something out of a horror film,' A visibly shaken Constable
Gardner would later tell the court in his evidence. 'I couldn't believe

my eyes. I've been in the police force for eleven years and never had to deal with anything like this.'

In the flat the police went to the bathroom and discovered body parts hidden behind a shower curtain. At first the officers thought what they were seeing were parts of a mannequin, but they quickly came to the shocking realisation that the arms and legs in the bath were human. The legs had been severed at the knees and there was also a saw in the shower. Christopher May, realizing his game was up, told the shocked policeman that there were other body parts hidden around the flat and elsewhere. He calmly directed police to a rucksack that contained the woman's torso.

May was immediately arrested and while the police cordoned off a large area around the man's flat, they were soon to realize that the situation they were dealing with was indeed like something out of a tacky horror film. The woman's head was later found in a storm drain close to the Pontypridd Rugby Club, and had May had more time he would have disposed of the rest of the body in a similar fashion. He would later tell the police that his reasoning behind placing the head in the storm drain was that heavy rain would wash it into the Rhondda river and from there out to sea. Though when May stood trial for the murder of Tracey Woodford, the prosecution suggested that May had placed the poor woman's head in the storm drain, balancing it on a ledge, so that he could visit it at a later date.

'I put them in a rucksack and carried them over,' May would tell the court when asked how body parts ended up in the drain. 'I hid them. I thought they would wash out into the sea.'

The body parts were not the worse of it. Investigations would reveal that Christopher May had calmly watched online pornography for several hours after strangling the woman, that he had likely engaged in sexual intercourse with the dead woman's body, and that he had flushed many of the woman's internal organs down the toilet.

Christopher May stood trial in November of that year, and his defence was that he had not murdered the woman, that he should not even face a charge of manslaughter but that this had been self-defence. 'Something terrible must have happened to induce this man [May] to do what he did,' Malcolm Bishop QC, told the jury in his summing up for the defence.

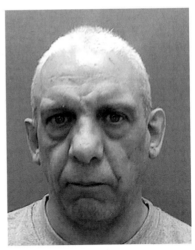

Christopher May in his police mug-shot. (*South Wales Police*)

May's story was that he and Tracey Woodford had left the pub together and gone back to his place. They had listened to music and drank several glasses of cider before going to bed where consensual sexual intercourse occurred. May said they then went to sleep, but he was awoken several hours later and saw Tracey standing besides the bed and going through his wallet. He shouted at her, telling the court he had called her a 'thieving bitch'. And then she attacked him and the next thing he knew was that the woman was dead. May said he had been in such a rage that he couldn't exactly remember what happened, but he stressed that he had not meant to kill the woman and when he realized what he had done he panicked which led to the dismemberment of the body. May had worked as a butcher many years previously and this was where the plan to cut up the body had come from. He had skills with knives, having spent many years cutting up animal carcasses, and although his plan was doomed to failure, May would claim that he had been acting in a state of shock over Tracey's death as the full enormity of what had happened sunk in.

The prosecution were having none of this and were able to establish, using May's internet history, that he had sat down and watched several hours of online pornography immediately following the murder.

This would hardly be the reaction of a man shocked and sickened by what had occurred in his flat. 'The killing of Tracey Woodford was sexually motivated and the details may cause horror and revulsion', the prosecution told the court. The prosecution would now make claims that May had performed sexual acts on the woman after she was dead, though the experts where unable to say exactly when the sexual intercourse had occurred, or if the woman had been alive at the time. The fact that May had been watching pornography following the murder suggested that he was at that point sexually aroused, which supported the prosecution's case.

Tracey Woodford. (*Author's collection*)

Christopher May would eventually be found guilty of murder and given a life sentence with a minimum term of twenty-eight years. Judge, Justice Nicola Davies told May that he was 'a dangerous sexual predator'. And before handing down the mandatory life sentence she told May that, 'You have fought this case from start to finish – and remorse has not been a feature of your defence. Your murder of Tracey Woodford was cruel, callous and determined. Those same characteristics prompted you to dismember the body of Tracey and then deliberately conceal it. This was done for one reason: to avoid detection of the murder you knew you had committed. You embarked on this with little thought for your victim and still less for her family whose grief for their daughter and sister was made more anguished by your grim dismemberment of the body.'

Chapter 14

Summing Up

The crime scene is the silent witness. The victim can't tell us what happened, so we need to give a hypothesis that explains what has taken place.

Peter Arnold, Crime Scene Investigator

The way police investigate crimes has changed dramatically in the time between the first and final cases featured in this book. All the way back in 1845, the year of the first case, forensic science was nothing less than science fiction, an unimagined advancement of a future impossibly distant. Fingerprinting, truly the foundation of forensic science, was not developed for use in criminal cases until the early years of the twentieth century and since then advancements have been rapid, with a million years worth of innovations being packed into the last century. The development of DNA technology for example is perhaps the single most important development in crime detection since the discovery that fingerprints could be used to establish identity.

In the opening months of 2016, an inquest was opened into an incredibly complex murder that took place back in 1997, but was not discovered until November 2015. Forensic sciences would play a large part in establishing what had happened, and DNA would be used to identify who the badly decomposed corpse had been.

The incredible facts in this case would turn the murder and concealment of John Sabine into one of the most remarkable in the history of violent crime. The story made front pages, not only locally but worldwide. It wasn't so much the method of killing, but more the realisation that the murdered man's wife had kept his body concealed in her home for all those years. Ann Sabine had embalmed the body, and wrapped it in thick plastic sheeting and tinfoil, and it was not until Mrs Sabine died that her grisly secret was finally revealed. So well hidden was the body that when she started a relationship with a new man, Derek Ellis, he was able to briefly move in with her and for some time they lived as a couple. It is incredible to think that Ann Sabine, even while living with another man, was able to keep her dark secret that somewhere in the house they shared was the hidden mummified body of her husband. When Derek Ellis died from liver disease in 2010, Ann remained single until her own demise.

'This is an extraordinary set of circumstances and we are working tirelessly to put together the pieces of what is a complex investigation.' Detective Chief Inspector Gareth Morgan told reporters after the discovery of the body. Ann Sabine lived in Beddau, a small Welsh village on the outskirts of Pontypridd. She had moved there in 1997, and soon established herself as a colourful member of the local community. She told neighbours that she had moved here from New Zealand, which was only one of the lies she had told. It would turn out that she had indeed lived in New Zealand, had emigrated there in the 1960s but, together with her husband John, had returned to Britain during the mid-1980s, abandoning their five children in New Zealand. She claimed to have been born in Australia but in reality her birthplace was Pentre in the Rhondda Valleys.

As soon as Ann moved into the former coal-mining village of Beddau she became something of a talking point. She had bleached blonde hair and usually dressed in youthful black, chain-smoked, and called everyone 'darling'. And at differing times claimed that she had once been a cabaret artist, a supermodel, a high-class prostitute, and had been married to a millionaire. Friends said that she seemed harmless enough and they took her eccentric claims with a pinch of salt.

It was in August of 2015 that Ann fell ill and was taken to hospital, where it was discovered that she was riddled with cancer. She returned home briefly and it was then that it is believed she removed the body from her home and hid it beneath a pile of rubbish in her well tended garden. Shortly afterwards Ann grew weaker and returned to hospital where she died on 30 October, taking her dark secret to the grave with her.

Ann Sabine. (*Author's collection*)

It was a neighbour, Michelle James, who discovered the grisly secret and for her troubles found herself arrested on suspicion of murder. Prior to Ann Sabine's death Michelle had become friendly with her and used to run errands for, as well as cooking as the woman's health deteriorated. During the time that Michelle was caring for Ann she heard many wild stories, once the woman had told her that she had been a medical student and that she had a medical skeleton. And following Ann's death Michelle noticed the large wrapped object on the compost heap and assumed it was this medical skeleton.

Michelle is a vivacious, fun-loving 41-year-old woman and she decided that it would be good to get the skeleton and play a prank on her boyfriend. She and a friend went into Ann's garden which was a communal plot that they all shared, and went to the package containing what she thought would be a medical skeleton.

Michelle and her friend had to cut through several layers of thick plastic, cardboard and tinfoil. The first indication that all was not as it should be came when the women detected a dreadful smell coming from the package. 'There was sludge inside,' Michelle would later tell police. 'And then I saw it was a dead body. I completely lost the plot and was in meltdown.'

Michelle immediately called the police only to find herself arrested on suspicion of murder. The police kept asking her who it was in the wrapping, questioning her about the boyfriends she had met through an internet dating site. They showed her pictures of the body once it had been removed from the packaging, and it could be clearly seen that the man's head was caved in. Michelle was then questioned about her ex-husband who had liver problems and she told police that she didn't know if he was alive or dead.

In all Michelle would spend four days in police custody before being released without charge, when DNA tests revealed that the body in the bag had been that of Ann Sabine's husband John who had not been seen since 1998. The police would come to believe that Ann Sabine had killed her husband with several blows to the head from a blunt instrument, had them embalmed the body, wrapped him in thick plastic and then concealed him in her two-bedroomed home for the best part of two decades. As the investigation wore on it would also be revealed that Ann had continued claiming her husband's pension and that she had thousands of pounds in their joint bank account.

Had it not been for the meticulous forensics work, then there is no doubt that Michelle would have gone onto face a jury on the charge of murder, as it was police were able to establish that Ann Sabine was in actual fact the killer, and that as soon as she'd realized she herself was dying she had moved the body outside the house. It was an incredible story, one better suited to the imagination of a fiction author. And yet it is often said that life is stranger than fiction and in the case of Ann Sabine this certainly rings true.

Select Bibliography

Newspapers
Cardiff Times
Evening Express
Rhondda Leader
South Wales Echo
Western Mail

Archives
Private papers
Court transcripts
The National Archive
South Wales Police

Books
I am indebted to all those who have written on criminal history and found many books invaluable during my research. Among the books I frequently revisited were:

Hawkins, Elaine, and Avril Evans, *A Dark Past* (Whitchurch Books, 2002).
Isaacs, Mark, *Foul Deeds and Suspicious Deaths in Cardiff* (Pen and Sword Books, 2009).
McCreey, Nigel, *Silent Witness* (Random House, 2013).
Milkins, Neil, *Every Mother's Nightmare* (Old Bakehouse Publications, 2008).

Index

Page numbers in italics refer to illustrations.